# VIRTUAL

# *Flips*

How to **escape** the 9 to 5 & Flip Houses from **anywhere** using only your LapTop!

BY Christopher Seder
VirtualFlips.com

Table of Contents

# Virtual Flips Forward

Do you want to learn how to start flipping houses all across the country without every leaving your house? What about learning how to create your own automated Virtual Flipping Machine that literally allows you to work just a few hours each week while cashing wholesale checks almost automatically.

"Willingness to change is a strength, even if it means plunging part of the company into total confusion for a while"
-Jack Welch

Before we jump in I want to tell you a quick story. This is the story of two brothers who where both real estate wholesalers.

## The Epic Adventure of 2 House Flipping Masters

Once upon a time, there lived two real estate wholesalers Victor Flips and Ornery Flips.  They both lived in the same small town called HouseVile, Montana.

Victor and Ornery where both full time real estate wholesalers. They focused 100% of their efforts day in and day out flipping houses and had a lot of fun doing it. They had their own business and could flip as many houses as they wanted as long as they where out hustling and making it happen.

 Every day they would meet up at their parents house for a nice dinner with the family and each HUGE meatballs and discuss how many houses they flipped that day.

**Life was awesome.**

Then one day Victor discovered something that would turn out to change his life forever. You see one day Victor was out flipping a house when on a coffee table inside the house he found a book called the "4-Hour Work week". Now at first he thought to himself 4 hour work week, want kind of garbage is this, sounds like something a lazy broke person would buy, everyone knows that if you want to make it in the flipping business you need to be out working 10 hours or more every day until your rich.

At first Victor just discarded the book but then after he checked the crawl space of the house he climbed out, all covered in cob webs and spiders he had a thought.  What if the book was actually legit?  I mean the cover is fancy and has a little guy lounging between two palm trees on it.

So Victor decided to peak inside the book and after just reading the first half of a page was hooked.  He immediately ran home that, literally left his car and ran like a jackrabbit.

You see Victor and Ornery where taught by their father to flip houses and they had only learned one way to wholesale houses and that was to do all of the work them selves.  They spent all of their time researching property, calling sellers, filling out contracts, looking at houses, inspecting property, finding buyers, and doing everything them selves.

**But as fate would have it this was all about to change.**

That night Victor did not show up to his parent's house for their normal meatball dinner.  Tonight was actually spaghetti and 2 X larger meatball night. Ornery got really worried at dinner because he knew how much Victor loved his meatballs.

After dinner and watching Hawaii Five-O with his parents Ornery decided he would go over to Victors house and see if everything was ok. Armed with a sack of meatballs he drove his old ford truck over there. His house was actually only a block away so he got there very fast.

When ornery got to victors house he found Victor sprawled out on his comfy couch with his face glued to a strange book. After several HEY Victors, ornery finally slapped Victor across the face with his sack of meatballs which got his attention.

Ornery asked "WHAT IN THE HECK IS GOING ON?" WHY DID YOU MISS DINNER? ARE YOU DYING? AND WHAT IS THAT WEIRD BOOK YOU ARE READING? AND WHY DO YOU DRESS LIKE A JIGALO?" Victor slowly put down the "4-hour work week" book and told ornery to sit down he had something Important to say to him.

Victor told ornery the story about how he found the book and once he started reading it he could not put it down even for 2x large meat balls. Victor told Ornery that this book might be the most important, game changing book he has ever read (the only other book he ever read in his life was Moby Dick).

Victor explained to Ornery how Tim Ferris the author in the book travels the world, works on a few hours each week and runs a business that brings in consistent income each and every month wither he is working or not.  And that you can apply the principals from the book to real estate wholesaling very easily and Flip houses every day like they already where but not have to work 10 hours a day. Ornery could not believe what he was hearing.  I mean, he knew Victor was always a dreamer but to think Victor had fallen this low to think that you can learn how to flip houses working less time was just down right crazy.

Ornery decided to take matters into his own hand and grabbed the book and threw it out the window. He said Now Victor you know this is just crazy talk; here are your meat balls I need to get going so I can wake up at 4:30 am tomorrow and get to work. Victor thought to himself good thing I ordered the audio version of the book with my amazon prime account.  So the next day Victor decided to take everything he leaned from reading the "4-Hour Work Week" 1 ½ times and put it into action.

He stared by creating a system for every part of his real estate wholesaling business, mapped everything out so he could easily teach someone to replace him.

Once he had all of the systems Victor build a team around himself and taught his team to do every aspect of his business. His team would even hand deliver his Wholesale checks daily to his doorstep. One week Victor didn't even get out of his bath robe, which really traumatized one of his team members who got to see a little more of Victor that he wanted to.

Over the course of just a few months Victor decided that he wanted to work a little more than just 2 hours a week which he had got his work load down to so he decided to create the same process he was using in HouseVille and duplicate it in HomeVille.

After another Month of work Victor had 2 successful automated wholesaling businesses up and running and he had still not changed from his bathrobe, which was getting very smelly.

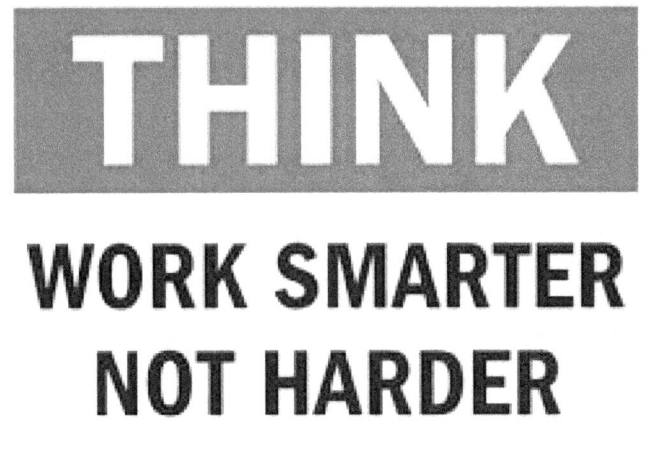

Later that day Victor decided he would go and eat some meatballs with his family.   That night at Dinner Ornery asked Victor how his wholesaling business had been going.  Victor explained to Ornery that he was now in 2 markets and flipped twice as many deals as he had before but has not really left his house in the past few months.

This really stumped Ornery and later that night they sat down together after "Hawaii Five-O" and Victor helped his brother realize that he was working Hard and not smart.   Over the next few months ornery also automated his entire business and Bought a bathrobe that matched Victors (minus the stains). From that day on Victor and Ornery both enjoyed a comfortable life where they never had to worry about money again, they traveled the world together deciding to do what they where ultimately passionate about and find that Dam Sasquatch.

They did find him the Mountains of Alaska.  Ornery ended up losing a finger in a tragic Sasquatch biting accident but we will save that for another story time.

**The End**.

What is the moral of the story? Most people think that in order to build a successful business, or to create wealth you must work 10 plus hours a day and never stop. Now with any business you must put in that hard work in the beginning but once you have a proven system in place like Victor and Ornery had there comes appoint where you must work smarter and not harder.

You must work on your business and not in your business. The Goal with any real estate investing business wither it be wholesaling, rehabbing or what ever is to create an actual business that can run without you.

# An Important Introduction Message from the Author: Christopher Seder

Congratulations! You're about to discover a practically unknown opportunity happening in cities all across the country right now. You made a very wise decision by investing in this book and more importantly investing in yourself. You're about to embark on an incredible journey and learn how you can create massive amounts of wealth through Virtual real estate wholesaling. This book is designed to help you quickly start making money with real estate wholesaling and join the ranks of the words brightest and best real estate investors.

This book is my own personal blue print for real estate investing and is what I use to train new employees, students and anyone that wants to learn the fastest way to put cash in their pocket. This book is going to help to lay a solid foundation for you. Within the pages ahead you are going to discover the strategies and principals that are working in today's real estate market.

I highly suggest you read every word of this book as you are going to learn how to finally get out of the RAT race and start creating financial for yourself and your family. So welcome! It's an honor to finally share what I believe is the easiest and best way for the average JOE to get started in real estate investing with very little money, no credit and no experience. Before I jump in I just want you to make me one promise, can you do that? Ok I trust you. The promise I want you to make me is that after reading through this book you ACTUALLY take some kind of action

## Who is Christopher Seder –The Virtual Flips Guy?

Before I jump showing you how you can easily cash fast checks each and every month working only a few hours doing it, I am sure you are thinking to yourself who the Heck is Christopher Seder and why should I care? So I am going to blabber a little bit about myself (makes me feel good inside), that way you know why I am uniquely qualified to write this book. First off, I am happy to admit that I am not an old timer who has been doing this business for year and year but I have grown up around real estate investing my entire life and Ill share that with you in a minute.

I am relatively young 29 years old at the time I am writing this but don't let my age fool you because I am a pretty darn savvy business man and real estate investor. I kind think it was my father's secret evil plan to turn me into a real estate investing genius (or make sure I was finically successful).

I began my real estate investing/wholesaling career almost straight out of college. After college I was ready to conquer the business world and started looking for a JOB.

Very soon after I started searching I started to see a common occurrence. Everywhere I looked the starting pay was somewhere around the $30,000 per year range. Maybe I was delusional but I thought I would be offered a 6 figure CEO job right out or college and work my away up in a year or two to 7 figures.

## What is my Purpose?

Anyway after looking at my options something odd hit me, I started thinking back to my child hood years an started to remember my father talking about consistently making $30,000 or more on small real estate flips and I remembered he did 2 or 3 a year. This is when I had my ah ha moment and realized why in the world would I want to work 60 hours per week and make $30,000 per year when I could make $30,000 doing one real estate flip that took only a few months to complete.

So I then decided to speak with my father who at the time had also accumulated around 80 rentals or cash flow machines, as I like to call them. After speaking with my father I then realized that real estate investing was my Destiny. I ended up deciding to go to work for my father as a SLAVE (handy man kind of) working on his rentals and learning the business from the ground up. As a side note if you want to learn any sort of business you need to be actively in the trenches sweating your ass off. After about 5 months or so of working on rentals, working on fix and flip projects and learning everything I could about real estate investing my father and I decided I was ready to go out and conquer the world and start my own real estate investing business.

## The Start of the Quest

After months and months of trying to really figure the game out I did finally end up closing my first wholesale deal where I was able to flip a house and cash a $13,000 wholesale fee.   That was the start of my real estate investing career and then after that nothing could stop me.   We started wholesaling more and more consistently and also I started partnering with my father and doing Fix and Flip projects where we were making $30,000 or more per deal.

And that leads me to where we are today, as of January 2015 we have made over $500,000 in the past year or so and just in the first part of January 2015 we are on track to make close to $40,000.    I have grown my business to do more than just wholesaling real estate, we buy rentals and also the bulk of our profits come from fix and flip deals but wholesaling is a source of consistent income in my business.   I mean there is no easier way to cash a $5,000 or $10,000 check.   I will explain in great detail what exactly wholesaling is later in this book.  It is the only strategy I know here you can work 4 hours on a deal and make that kind of money.  I have literally working 4 hours on a wholesale deal and cashed a $7,800 check.   That is like $1,900 per hour.   We have a deal closing next Tuesday actually where we will be making close to $9,000 on it and honestly I may have 2 hours total of work put into it.

## The Struggle is Real

Even though I had an experienced real estate investor (my father) to guide me I still struggled to really get going. The reason was because I was not educated; I did not know what to do or even how to talk to people about buying their house. This is why it is very important to learn as much as you can and then just DIVE in and star making it happen. Even though my father had been an experienced real estate investor for 30 plus years his business was very unique in the fact that he did zero marketing. His 2 or 3 rehabs he bought a year came from people knowing what he did and just referring the deals to him.

For me this did not work, I was not experienced and I wanted to generate and do more than 2 or 3 deals a year. I needed to go out and learn everything I could about marketing for sellers and finding deals. I quickly learned that MOST real estate investors suck at marketing. Once I tested and found what worked best in my area (vacant houses and yellow letters), I started having massive amounts of success and leads starting pouring in like crazy.

Let me also jump back really quick, I know I am kind of all over the place in this intro about me section but random thoughts and crap keep coming into my head and why not add it here. Another random point is that I want to express that I am not a professional writer, my grammar stinks, I cant spell (small town education), and what the heck is a punctuation? With that said please do not focus on my errors but focus on the message.

Ok back to my ramblings, one of the HUGE keys to my success in being able to actually start making consistent income with real estate wholesaling and investing was when I was able actually QUIT my regular JOB. When I was getting started I had to actually work another JOB to pay the bills. I worked as an independent contractor property inspector for a few different banks.

What I would do was drive around and takes pictures of Bank owned property, pre-foreclosures and do insurance inspections. Now this job was pretty good in the fact that I was able to look at houses all day long but it was also bad in the fact that 50 hours a week I spent doing work for someone else which left little time for me to actually work on my real estate investing business.

## Working for the Man Sucks

I was actually a total slave to this company and was kind of stuck. They would give me orders I would have to complete in just a few days or I would not get paid and had me running around like a chicken with my head cut off.

For most people a JOB where most of your time is spent building someone else's empire prevents you from having anytime to build your own. This is why I am a strong believer in the sink or swim method of real estate investing. Sink or swim means that you pretty much quit your job and go full time into real estate investing and leave yourself no other option but to succeed. You either start making money and making deals happen or you go broke.

Most people that are backed up to a corner and MUST make it happen actually succeed. When there is no pressure and you are in your comfort zone (your job), you are less likely to really make it happen. When I deceived enough was a enough I did not have a reserve of money sitting there for me, I had enough for a few months but I knew if I did not take a shot I would be stuck in the rat race forever and I might never get out.

Now I have hundreds of thousands in the banks, have 15 rentals bringing in passive income each month, I am doing 2 or 3 rehab projects a month, and also wholesaling houses all across the country. Life is getting easier and easier each and every day and I have real estate investing to thank for that.

**I created my Own Real Estate Money machine!**

I know you may think I am a little crazy for telling you to quit your JOB and dive in headfirst. For some people this is the only way they will ever succeed in real estate investing. For others it might not be the best strategy. In this book I am going to show you a proven way where you can create your own real estate money machine that produces a consistent $5,000, $10,000 or more in income each and every month.

I was able to accomplish more in my first year of going full time then most people accomplish in decades or doing real estate investing part time or half assed as I like to refer to it.

I was not able to accomplish this because I am a genius or anything. I was able to do this because I started consistently doing time tested and proven foundational real estate investing principals. The key to my business was and still is consistency. If you want to succeed you need to be doing what is necessary to generate deals consistently.

In this book I am also going to share with you what works and what does not work so you can focus 90% of your effort on what actually brings in deals and not waste your time consistency doing crap that does not work. Anyone can duplicate what I've done and start making money with real estate investing in the next 30 to 60 days.

**Why is my Rambling Story important to you?**

Because whether you know a lot or are brand new to real estate investing there is still always something to learn. Every day I am always testing and tweaking new marketing ideas and learning form my successes and mistakes. It is important that you look at other successful people who have come before you look at the mistakes they have made and not make the same mistakes. It is also important that you copy what successful people are doing and implement it in your own business.

I am not trying to say everything I do is correct or that I am the best. I have figured out how to consistently make money in real estate investing and I want to share with you what is truly possible when it comes to wholesaling real estate. You are going to have to try things out for your self, make mistakes and continue to learn and improve your business. Not everything that I talk about will be what is best for you but that is the beauty of real estate investing there are so many different niches that you can choose what is best for you.

**What your about to Learn**

You're about to learn how to become one of the best real estate wholesalers in your area or in any area in the United States. You can take what you learn in this book and apply it to your own real estate market or apply it to any real estate market across the country.

You'll discover an easy to follow step-by-step method for going out and making a fortune wholesaling houses earning anywhere from $5,000 to $10,000 or more per deal. You will learn how you can create your own wholesaling business locally or create your own Virtual Wholesaling business all across the country. I am currently wholesaling in several markets across the U.S., which I will get to more as we process through this book.

As you read through this book remember to take notes, highlight this book and re-read chapters. Your going to learn a lot of information and it might take a couple readings to fully understand everything.

So…Are you ready?  Let's get started….

# Notes:

# Chapter One: The Journey Begins NOW!

"No person will make a great business who wants to do it all himself or get all the credit"
-Andrew Carnegie

Now that you have a little bit of background on me it is time to start laying your education foundation. It is important that you fully understand what exactly wholesaling is and all of the terms and things that go a long with it. I want to make sure that even the beginner that has never heard of wholesaling can understand what is after this next chapter. If your experienced and already know what wholesaling is DO not skip this chapter, I am going to share with you a few important stories.

## How do we make money?

The two most common ways most people think that real estate investors make money is by buying, fixing up and re-selling ugly houses. You know like they do on TV in shows like flip this house, flipping Vegas, flip or flip, flipping Boston and what not. My main business is Fixing and Flipping houses because that is where the BIG money can be made and where I want you to strive to get. But for beginners just are getting started I do not recommend you start fixing and flipping houses.

The second common way most people think of making money with real estate investing is being a land lord. Buying a nice rental property and having a renter who pays you passive income each month. I am also buying a couple houses each year that I add to my rental portfolio but rentals are also not the best way for a new investor to start. Rentals can be great for passive income but they can also take a lot of time, work and stress. Once you have built up a stock pile of money and have more experience start buying a few rentals here and there to see if its for you. Some people love it and others hate it. So that brings us to the topic of this book, wholesaling real estate.

## What is real estate wholesaling?

Wholesaling Houses is technically just playing middleman or matchmaker. It is the business of finding great deals on real estate (wholesale deals), putting the property under contract and then quickly assigning that deal to a Fix and flip buyer or Land lord. You make a small market up between $1,000 and $20,000 or more sometimes. Putting the property under contract means signing a PURCHASE and SALE agreement to buy the property.

**So here is a quick wholesaling formula to help you understand a little better. It is a hard concept to grasp sometimes.**

1. You find a Motivated Seller (someone willing to sell you the property at a discount) and you negotiate a sales price around 40% to 60% of the After Repair Value or market value.

2. Next you take that price say you put a $100,000 house under contract for $50,000 (50%) and you then mark it up $5,000 to $55,000

3. You then market that property to local real estate investors in your area (we will get to how you do this)

4. Once you find a buyer you simply assign your contract to them for a $5,000 or what ever you want assignment fee.   You take the contract and assignment to the title company and they start the closing process and then in just a few weeks you have your $5,000 assignment check

What do you think?  If your still confused google wholesaling real estate or wholesaling houses and start reading and watching YouTube videos.  The Internet has so much info out there.

As you can see wholesaling is not very complicated and there really is only a few simple steps to follow. Once you can master all of the steps it become a piece of cake to flip houses working only a few hours. Now to start off it might take a little more work and effort until you learn and figure out your own system.

## What is Virtual Wholesaling?

Ok so I want to make sure you also under stand one of the main focuses of this book and that is virtual wholesaling. Most people when they think of Virtual Wholesaling they think of someone like myself living in Montana and flipping houses in places like Florida. AKA someone flipping houses in a market they Do not live in.

Now that is very true but I want you to understand that you can also flip houses virtually in your own real estate market. Yes this is how I personally run my wholesaling business in my local market also, I don't go out and look at houses, I don't talk to very many sellers (sometimes), and I typically don't meet with buyers anymore. I have everything automated to the point where I don't really have to leave my office or house anymore.

To run my virtual wholesaling business I have put together a good solid team (me and an acquisitions manager, and Boots on the Ground in other markets). For you to start all you need is yourself and then learn how to put your team in other markets together as you go.

## Wholesaling vs. Rehabbing aka Fixing and Flipping

Now I know what you are probably thinking, why don't I just figure out how to buy the house and make HUGE money rehabbing instead of wholesaling?   The big thing about wholesaling is that there is virtually ZERO risk as appose to rehabbing where there is HUGE risk.   Wholesaling you can make cash in just a few weeks where rehabbing it takes months and months.

Believe me there is a lot less of a headache wholesaling.   You do not have to deal with a lot of contractors not showing up for work and trying to over charge you for crappy work.   But wholesaling is a great way for you to start learning from other experienced investors who have their rehabbing systems down.   You will be the one who is out finding them killer deals and they will love you for it.

# Why does the world need wholesalers?

Wholesalers provide not only a source for killer real estate deals for landlords and also rehabbers but they also help out motivated sellers who NEED to sell their house.   There are thousands of if not millions of people all across the united states who have ugly distressed properties they no longer want, these are people who desperately need out of what seems like a "terrible" situation.

Wholesalers are helping these motivated sellers find solutions to their problems.  Most sellers hid in a hole until someone like us contacts them and shows them there is a better way.   If there were not wholesalers out there telling people with distressed properties that they have options a lot of these people would lose their home or it would end up falling into so much disrepair it would just have to be torn down.

## Advantages of Wholesaling Houses

Some people view wholesaling as a stepping-stone to bigger and better real estate opportunities.  It can be but it also can be a highly profitable business that you can automate.   Some days I personally think that I should only focus on wholesaling houses and stop doing rehabs.
On rehabs I usually make around $30,000 and on wholesale deals I usually make around $5,000, So why on earth would I want to do smaller deals.

Well it all boils down to the amount of time and effort I put in. When doing a wholesale deal I normally put in around 4 to 5 hours of work. That is it. On rehabs I usually spend more like 80 hours. I am consistently checking on projects, getting material, making sure workers are working, talking with contractors about change orders, ordering crap, showing the property, qualifying buyers and so on. It really does turn into a lot of work.

If I am working 5 hours to make $5,000 I am making $1,000 per hour as a pose to working 80 to 160 hours to make $30,000 I am making $375 to $187.50 per hour. Now that is still great money but why not what do is easiest. If I did 20 wholesale deals in a year and made $100,000 and only worked 100 hours I could spend the rest of my time enjoying life with my family. But if I did 10 rehabs and made $300,000 but had to work 1,600 hours 16x my life is a lot busier. You can see why wholesaling can be a much easier option for some.

Just a quick side note: I can wholesale houses working about 4 or 5 hours because I have experience and systems in place that allow me to do that. Most beginners might have to work 10 or 20 hours on one wholesale deal, until they build up their business and experience.

## Killer Money, and Low Low Risk

I have already touched on this a little bit but wholesaling real estate is one of the lowest risk investment strategies you can do. Because you are not actually buying the property or taking ownership you're not taking a huge risk at all.

 You are the middleman between the seller and the buyer and in most cases you never put down any of your own money, your end buyer puts down all of the money.

You do not have any holding cost, closing cost, or anything.   You also are in an out of the property in less than 30 days, which allows you to do more deals then if you were doing rehabs.

## Is wholesaling illegal?

Some people think that wholesaling real estate is acting as a real estate Broker without a license, which is illegal.  Let me be very clear with you wholesaling houses is not illegal but I do see some wholesalers doing illegal things which would constitute they are trying to Broker houses without a real estate license. You do not need a license to sell house but you do need to follow a few basic laws.

# LEGAL

First in order to sell a house you need to either have a listing agreement on it (and be a realtor), own the property or have an equitable interest in the property. Because we are wholesaling property and never actually taking an ownership interest in the property we need to acquire an equitable interest in the home.

**How do we do this?**

In order to get an equitable interest in the property all you need to have is some sort of real estate purchase and sale agreement signed with the owners or an option contract on the property and then you are free to market and sell your interest.
There you have it, if any uneducated realtors or people say its illegal for you to wholesale houses you can tell them the actual truth.

**Do you have any questions?**

I hope that I have covered the basics of wholesaling pretty well. The rest of this book we will dive into everything you need to do in order start making a lot of money with real estate investing.

The key to remember is that no matter what the real estate market is doing wither its up, down, or flat there will always be real estate investors buying and selling houses.  There will always be a need for wholesalers who can go out and find discounted property in any real estate market.

Right now is one of the very best times in history to get started in wholesaling houses.  There are more people buying and selling houses so the demand for people that can easily find cheap houses for rehabbers and landlords is huge.

Despite what you will hear in the media and from friends today's environment is prime for us.  You are in the right place at the right time.

Now are you ready to get more in depth into real estate wholesaling and learn more about the fun and exciting world of real estate investing?
Remember if you have any in-depth questions about real estate investing feel free to ask me at
**VirtualFlips.com**

# The Overview of our Virtual Flips Business

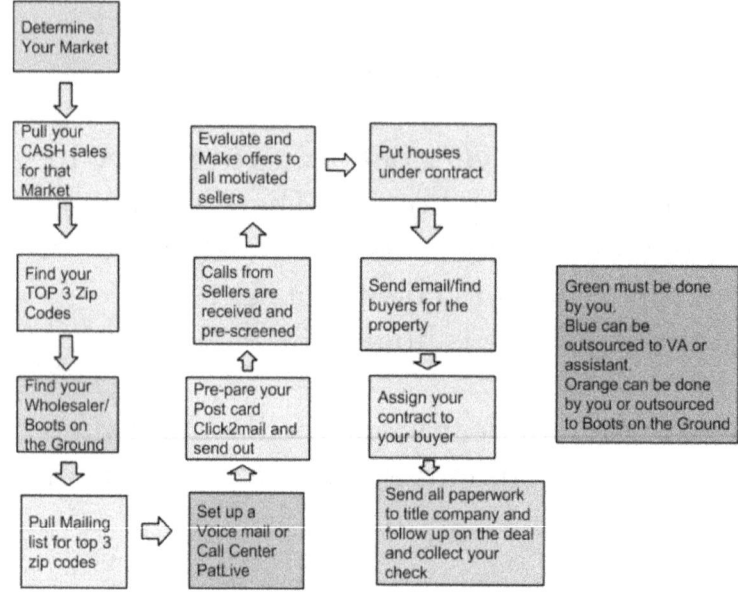

This is the Business Overview this book will focus on each stage of our entire process. Each Chapter we will focus on a new section. You can do this in almost any market across the country.

1) Start with Determining the Right real estate market (market research)

2) Analyze the market you picked by pulling cash sales and picking the very best areas to start wholesaling in.

3) Find your Boots on the Ground/Wholesaler to do 90% of your work

4) Set up and Send out your marketing

5) Receive Phone calls-Prescreen and send to your wholesaler

6) Wholesaler Evaluates the deal and makes and offer puts houses under contract
7) Send emails and Find a buyer for the property (wholesale does)
8) Send all the paperwork to the title company and close the deal.

Now lets dive into more detail and break down the pieces in to easy to digest processes.

**Random Things YOU must learn or look like a dumbass**

Before we dive into the nuts and bots of wholesaling real estate I think it's important that you learn a few basic real estate concepts. These are things that you will come across and people in the real estate world will talk about. If you do not learn them you may have to ask people questions and I know how some people (men) don't like to ask questions because they may feel stupid.
If you have read about real estate investing or been an active real estate investor most of these concepts will be failure to you. But if you're brand new this will be a great section to get you up to speed with common terms and formulas. This will be a quick overview chapter.

   ✓ **After Repair Value** - ARV this is what a property is worth when its fixed up and in 100% move in ready condition.

- ✓ **Retail Value** - This is another term that can means after repair value.  This is what the property will sell for if put on the open market and purchased by a RETAIL buyer.  Someone who will be living in the home.  Retail does not have to always mean 100% fixed up because some buyers will pay a Retail price for even fixed uppers.   Retail for a fixer upper would be ARV –Repairs =Retail value.   This is because RETAIL buyers are not looking for lots of equity to make a profit.
- ✓ **Comparable Sales** –Comps are recent house sales that are similar in size, location and style to the house you are looking to buy.   Put your Comps together to determine what the ARV is.
- ✓ **Assessed Value** –Value the city puts on a property for tax purposes.  This is not the TRUE value of the house just what is used to determine taxes.  Use comps for ARV.
- ✓ **Maximum Allowable Offer (moa)-** This is a formula used by most real estate investors to determine what the MAX you can pay for a property.  The formula can be found in the pre-screening and evaluating section.
- ✓ **CASH on Cash Return** – This is a formula that most landlords use to determine if a property is good for a rental or not.   Net Revenue/Cash Invested =Cash on Cash Return.

- ✓ **Income Approach** -The income approach is like the cash on cash return its also another formula to determine the value of an income producing rental property. Google for more info.
- ✓ **Appraisals** –An appraisal is used to determine the After repair value of a property. Its used by realtors and banks to determine it. We as wholesalers just use comps.
- ✓ **Motivated Sellers** – A motivated seller is someone who needs to sell a house because of either financial distress or has a property in physical distress.
- ✓ **Earnest Money** –Small deposit you put up when entering a real estate contract. Typically between $10 and $500. Some will require up to 1% of the total purchase price.
- ✓ **Inspection period** -Period of time where you can inspect the property and have the right to cancel your contract.
- ✓ **Purchase and Sale Agreement** –This is a contract you sign with a seller when buying or wholesaling a property.
- ✓ **Assignment Contract** -1 page document used to assign your right to purchase a property to another real estate investor.
- ✓ **Private Lenders** –A private individual who funds real estate deals for investors.

- ✓ **Hard Money Lenders** – These lenders lend to real estate investors at a high interest rate and usually lend at 65% of the ARV or less. Interest rates are typically 15 to 18%.
- ✓ **Transactional Funding** -Gap funding you can use to purchase a property and sell the property either the same day or within a few days.
- ✓ **Joint Venturing** –Partnering on real estate transactions.
- ✓ **Direct Mail** –Mail you send out directly to a seller.
- ✓ **Real Estate closing** -A closing is when you or your buyer and seller sign all of the legal documents to transfer ownership of a property.
- ✓ **Title companies** – Title companies handle real estate closing. They prepare all of the documents, deeds and do all of the title research.
- ✓ **Closing Attorneys** –Closing attorneys are used instead of title companies in some states. They do the same work as title companies.

Now lets Dive in to Step 1 of setting up your virtual flips business so you can get out and flip a house.

# Chapter 2: The Corner Stone of your Business –Market Research

" Real Estate Investors who ignore market research are as dangerous as an armed Hand grenade in the hands of an enemy"
–Christopher Seder

Have you ever just randomly started digging up your back yard looking for buried treasure or gold?  Have you ever-just drove out into the middle of a field and starting drilling for oil?

No of course not that would be silly.  If you want to strike oil you need to know where the best oil rich grounds are right?  The same goes for treasure and gold.  If you want to find treasure you will follow a treasure map or if you want to find gold you will do your research and find where you are most likely to strike it rich.

The same thing applies to real estate wholesaling. We do not just go out and look where ever for deals because every neighborhood is different and every town is different. The key to being successful is knowing where the very best areas in your town are. The areas where you are all but guaranteed to find a consistent stream of killer real estate deals and areas where you know people want to buy.

The number one key to becoming a successful virtual flipper is to pick the right real estate markets to go into. You can either go about wholesaling the hard way which is going at it blind and just picking a market because you saw on TV that it's a hot market or you can do it the correct way and pick your real estate market based on Cold hard facts.

In order to do that you must do your market research. In this report we have DONE the first step in market research for you.

The first step in market research is finding the best markets across the United States that has a good amount of CASH sales and a Good amount of inventory.   Every market is going to be different and have its own challenges but that is the fun of real estate wholesaling.

## How do you determine which cities are the best to go into?

In order for a real estate market to be potentially good or bad for real estate wholesalers we want to look at HOW many investors are purchasing and also look at the amount of supply on the market.   This gives us an idea of how successful we will be in a given real estate market.

Ideally we want to focus our efforts in areas where our efforts as a wholesaler are going to be very very easy.   Which means it will be easy for us to find deals and also easy for use to sell the deals.

## There are three kinds of real estate markets we look at.

### Competitive real estate markets
These are markets where there are a lot of people purchasing right now and inventory has shrunk.   In competitive markets it will be harder to find good solid deals but when you do find them it very easy to sell the houses.

## Average Real Estate markets

I call the middle real estate markets average because we find there will be a good solid mix of deals available and a good solid amount of cash buyers looking to buy the deals.

This is where we wan to focus our efforts.

## Inventory Rich Areas

The third type of real estate market is the inventory rich market. This is where there is an abundance of inventory but not very many buyers. In these places you can find hundreds and hundreds of deals but because there are so many deals wholesalers are not always needed, and buyers can pretty much cherry pick the best deals all day long. These areas would include places like Detroit and Pittsburg. Where you can literally buy houses for $1 but NO one wants them.

The **Middle is your Average Spot and where we want to focus**. Some markets will be boarding on the edge of Competitive and Inventory Rich but as long as you focus on markets that are somewhat close to the Middle you will have success.

Lots of Buyers (highDemand)   Lots of Deals (over supply)

# Step 1: How to Pick the Very Best City to Start in

The First thing we wan to look at when picking a new city is Population. Logic tells us that the larger the population the more opportunity there is right? Well that is halfway correct.

## So first lets analyze 4 real estate markets together

Let's look at my area Billings MT lets also look at Denver Colorado, Atlanta GA and Cleveland OH.

| | Population | Realtor.com Listings | City Listings | Absentee Sales | Com A | Com B |
|---|---|---|---|---|---|---|
| ✓ | Cleveland: 2,000,000 | 13,180 | 7,000 | 753 | 13,180 | 753 |
| ✓ | Billings MT: 160,000 | 780 | 630 | 103 | 9,750 | 1,288 |
| ✓ | Denver CO: 2,700,000 | 5,560 | 1,380 | 1,567 | 4,119 | 1,161 |
| ✓ | Atlanta GA: 5,500,000 | 20,000 | 4,800 | 542 | 7,272 | 197 |

Com A =Comparison of Inventory reatlor.com listings comparing if markets where the same size
Com B= Comparison of Sales if markets where the same size.

Now looking at the populations, amount of listings which market would you choose to go into? Which market looks like it has a good amount of inventory and a good amount of sales?

If you answered Cleveland you would be correct. As you can also see Billings MT if it was bigger in size would be a great market for wholesaling houses in. The problem with smaller markets is you are still limited by the amount of inventory available.

As a rule of thumb for virtual wholesaling I like to stick with markets that have a population of above 500,000 but if your own market is less than that don't let that stop you. We still buy several houses each month in our own market and smaller markets around us.

So what you can do is analyze 10 to 20 real estate markets and look at which markets you think might be best.

## STEP 2 In Market Research –Diving Deep

The next step in market research is to determine the very best areas in the market you are going to be wholesaling in.

- **War Zones:** You will want to stay away from war zones. Prices will be very cheap in these areas and you can probably make good money flipping houses in these areas. I will not do business somewhere where I do not feel safe.

- **Working class:** The working class neighborhood is our favorite place to do deals. Homes in this area are affordable, have stable neighborhoods, and are safe. Working class is the best place for rentals; you can usually buy houses cheap enough so they will cash flow.

- **Middle Class:** These neighborhoods are where a lot of first time home buyers go. They are a great place for rehabbers and wholesalers.

- **High Income:** For the beginning investor I recommend you stay away from high end homes. An experienced investor can make hundreds of thousands flipping a high end home, but there is of course more risk involved.

In order to do this we want to pull all of the cash sales from the MLS for a metro area. When pulling cash sales we are looking for areas where there is a High amount of sales, at a fair price point. We want to avoid the ghetto areas and avoid the high-end areas.

When starting out you want to contact a real estate agent in the area and have them pull ALL of the cash sales from their MLS for the past 4 to 5 months. Depending on the area this can be a list anywhere from 600 to over 3,000. I say the more the better because your data will be better.

If you need a tutorial on how to pull cash sales from the MLS I have a video you can watch or send to your real estate agent so he knows what to do.

http://www.christopherseder.com/pulling-cash-sales/

With the cash sales we need to have necessary info like Address, City, State, ZIP, Beds, Bath, Sq ft and SOLD price.

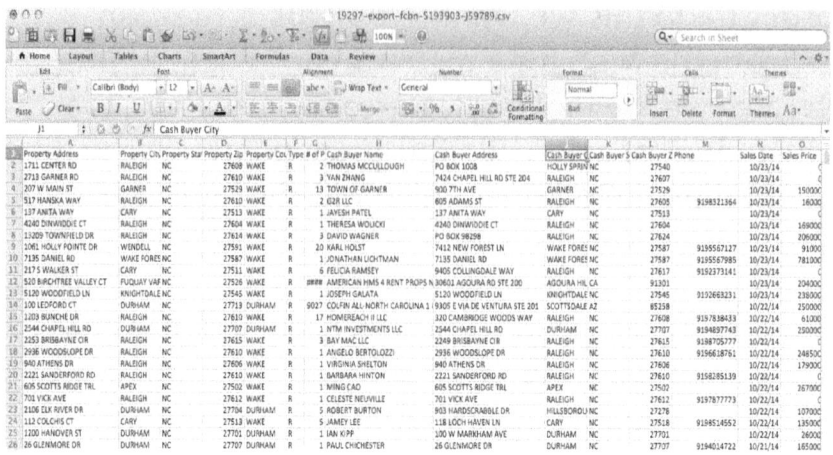

The data will either come in PDF format and you will have to convert it into an excel file (Google how to do this) or the data will come in an excel file which is the preferred method for sorting it.

Once you have the data you job now is to sort it inside excel by zip codes.    If you are not proficient with excel I suggest you start Googling how to videos.

I also use a software called Pin Pointer Pro which does the sorting for me and puts the info in a cool like map format like the picture below.

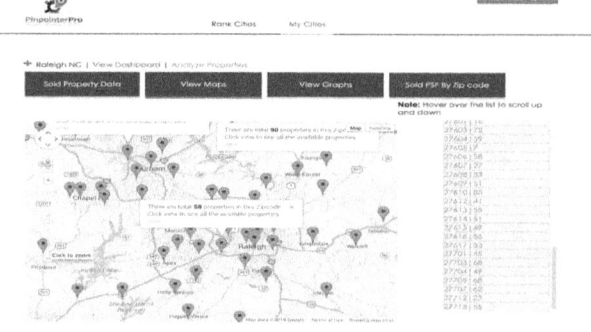

Ok so once the data is sorted you need to look through all of the zip codes and pick your top 5 or so. Look for areas where there are lots of sales and also at a fair price point.   Like I said you want to avoid the very low areas and also avoid the High priced areas.  Stick with the middle ground.

I personally like areas where I can pick up houses between $20,000 and $60,000 all day long.   I like these areas because you will find an abundance of land lords looking to buy and the price is low enough where they can easily cash flow a property.
Also if you want to map your cash sales data check out **Google Maps Engine**

https://Mapsengine.google.come/map

This is a really cool software you can use to upload all of your sales and then search them in the maps and see what people are paying in different areas of your town.

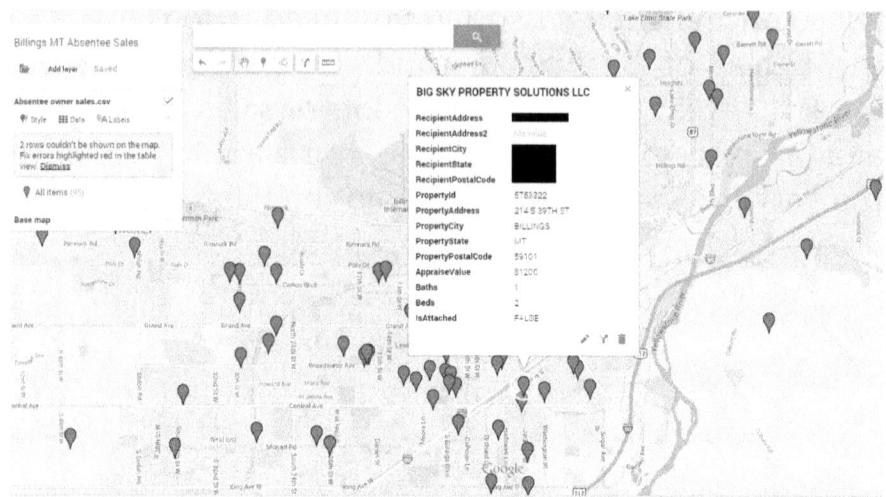

Ok so once you have your top 5 areas picked now your job with market research is pretty much done.  Your next step is going to be to build your team and then get your marketing sent out.

# Chapter 3: Building an Unstoppable Team

"Talent wins games, but teamwork and intelligence win championships."
*--Michael Jordan*

"Teamwork is the ability to work together toward a common vision. The ability to direct individual accomplishments toward organizational objectives. It is the fuel that allows common people to attain uncommon results."
*--Andrew Carnegie*

To become the King or Queen of the virtual wholesaling you need to build a team around you. Because a lot of our deals are Virtual in markets over 1,000 miles away we cannot go and look at every property we flip and honestly I don't want to.

I don't even want to look at houses 15 minutes from my house anymore unless they are going to be HUGE profit rehab deals.   Otherwise my team handles everything and I sit back and wait to collect a check.

When running a business the highest and best use of your time is actually RUNNING and growing the business and not working on very little aspect in the business.   I encourage you to pick up the book the E-MYTH.  This book will change your perspective on growing any type of business.   In the E-Myth the author talks about how the Job of a business owner is to work on the business and not in the business and to hire the right people to run the day-to-day operation.

I do encourage you to work in your business in the beginning and DO every aspect of the Job to a point where you have it down.   This way you can easily put everything you do into systems and teach someone how to do what is necessary in your business.

In my virtual wholesaling business I personally do not have any employees, but I have people that work for me on straight commission and get a piece each wholesale deal we do.   This way I can keep my expenses low and the people I work with are motivated to work hard in order to earn their paycheck.

I highly suggest you DO not hire any salary or by hour employees especially when starting out. It's best with real estate investing to pay them on each successful closing.

Another important reason why you should build a team around you is because with a team you can do twice as many deals and work less.

I have been able to do more wholesale deals over the past year because of the team I have in place. There is only so much time in the day and if all of my time was spent talking to sellers, looking at houses, evaluating deals, talking to buyers, etc. I would still do a lot of deals but if I were to take a vacation or day off nothing would happen in my business. You see this is another reason why you need a team around you. What happens if you want to take a months vacation? If its just you then NO income will come in and when you get back you will have to work harder than ever to make it up.

When building a team let's talk about some of the people you need to have.

I am going to focus on just virtual wholesaling when building a team but this same philosophy can be applied to your own local real estate market.

# Your Dream Team

**A real estate agent**
One of the very first people you will want to contact is good solid real estate agent in the area you want to start investing in. The main reason we need a real estate agent is to first help us do market research. In module one we talked about having a realtor pull all of the cash sales for us.

Ideal Candidate: Look for a realtor that has experience working with real estate investors, is comfortable making lots of offers and works for a smaller brokerage. Sometimes big brokerages or national brands like a Keller Williams can be difficult to work with.

**A Wholesaler/Boots on the Ground**

Because you will be wholesaling houses in other markets you need someone on the ground that can talk to sellers, go look a house, take pictures, show the property to buyers and do a variety of other things.

I personally like to work with experienced wholesalers because they know the business and know how to deal with sellers, and should already have an extensive buyers list.

Ideal Candidate: An experienced wholesaler who has been wholesaling houses full time for at least 1 to 2 years. Currently do 1 to 3 deals a month in their own business. Has a good reputation and has the same wholesaling philosophy as us.

**An Acquisitions Manager**
An acquisitions manager is someone that pretty much does all of the lead processing, negotiating, meeting with sellers, assessing property, and putting houses under contract. All of the legwork to get houses locked up. In the beginning this will be your job. Once you learn the process and can do it successfully you will want to hire out a commissioned acquisitions manager.

I pay ours $2,000 to $5,000 on houses we are going to buy our selves and pay 40 to 50% of wholesale fees. I pay them generously because they are doing most of the work.

Ideal candidate: A person with sales or negotiation background. Some real estate agents can make perfect acquisitions managers.

Experience is not a huge deal because you will be working closely with them.  Just need a self-motivated person, who is willing to learn and work hard.

## A Title Company

A title company makes sure that the title to a piece of real estate is legitimate and issues title insurance for the property.  They check to make sure there are not leans against the property or if there is gives you solutions on how to fix them.  Title companies handle real estate closings for real estate investors and realtors; they will handle all of the document preparation and everything.

Ideal Candidate: The best title companies to work with are ones that have worked with real estate investors before.  They know contract assignments, double closings and creative real estate solutions.  Find these types of title companies by talking with other wholesalers.

## Real Estate Attorney

A real estate attorney can serve several purposes. In some states all real estate closings happen at a real estate attorneys office instead of at a title company. They handle title reports, and all of the document preparation. A good real estate attorney can also help with legal issues that arise.

Ideal Candidate: An attorney that has worked with investors in the past, knows the real estate investing and wholesaling world. Is main business is real estate.

## Where do you find your team?

The very best way to start putting a team together is by asking for referrals, networking with others (over the internet), and just asking a lot of questions. When I say a lot I mean a lot, you want to really pre-screen the people you will be working with to make sure they are legit, cool people, and someone you would want to go grab a beer with. Working with people you think are cool or fun makes your life easier, you will not be

To find experienced wholesalers one of the very best places I have found good solid JV partners is in the Facebook Group "Wholesaling Houses Full Time". This group is one of the largest and most active real estate wholesaling groups around. With all business arrangements you must do your due diligence and make sure you are working with a Legit businessperson who has experience and is not a scumbag.

A great place to also find good wholesalers, title companies and even real estate agents is a local real estate investors association in the area. Most major cities have some kind of REIA.

Go to NationalREIA.com to find a reia in the area you want to flip in. Simply call them up and ask them for referrals.

The third place you will want to look for building your team is the top-secret web site Google. If your looking for a wholesaler simply Google terms like "We Buy Houses Area", "Wholesale real estate area", etc. You will find a bunch of them. You can also do the same for real estate agents and just start calling around. It may take you up to 10 phone calls to find a real estate agent who will actually get a good solid realtor who will pull the cash sales for you.

## How to Structure your Partner Ship with your Wholesaler?

There are 3 different ways you cans structure your joint venture with your wholesaler/Boots on the ground. Your experience level and trust with your potential partner will depend on how you structure the partnership.

1. The first way to I like to structure a Joint venture is a 50/50 split on wholesale fees. With this structure I handle all of the Direct mail marketing, prescreen the seller calls using my Pat live call center and then forward all of the calls to the wholesaler who does the rest of the work. He calls back sellers, sets appointments, puts houses under contract, finds buyers and manages the closing process. Once the property closes he sends me a check and we start over.

One reason why I like this strategy is that I can truly work only a couple hours on each deal and make a couple thousand in the process. But you have to have full trust with your wholesaler partner because once you send them the leads they will have full control over the process and could easily cut you out if they are a scumbag.

2.   The second way I like to structure a partnership is where I do the same process in the beginning, send out the marketing, receive the calls with my call center and then either I call all of the sellers back and negotiate a contract and I personally put the houses under contract. From that point on the wholesaler than goes and looks at the property, puts a lock box on and starts showing to potential buyers and then we manage the closing process. With this structure we have a payment split of either 60/40 or 70/30 depending on what you can negotiate with the wholesaler.

This can be a good strategy because you are more in control and can make sure you do not get cut out of any deals.

3.   And the 3rd way we structure a joint venture is by not using a wholesaler at all but instead using a real estate agent to represent us.   We structure realtor Joint ventures where they get 30% of our gross wholesale fee.   Its pretty much the same scenario as number 2, where they do all of the leg work, but the realtor also manages the closing process.

Here is a little section pulled from my Joint venture agreement.

## OBLIGATIONS OF THE JOINT VENTURERS:

The obligations of _____(you), as a Joint Venturer of this Agreement shall be, but are not limited to, the following:

- Market for Sellers using direct mail and the Internet.

- Pre-screen seller leads using Pat Live, Google Voice or a Virtual Assistant.

- Emailing/ forwarding seller leads

- Putting Property under contract

The obligations of _____Boots on the Ground_____, as a Joint Venturer of this Agreement shall be, but are not limited to, the following:

- Call back and meet with potential sellers.

- Putting the property under contract

- Marketing the property to cash buyers and selling the property

- Managing the closing process of the property.

Because we want to work the least amount as possible our goal is to find a legit wholesaler who can pretty much do 90% of the work for us. Our job will be to set up the marketing and sit back and let the wholesaler put the deals together and send us a check.

**Typical Deal**

Here is how our process works. We typically send out 1,000 to 2,000 post cards to a targeted area. From 1,000 to 2,000 post cards we will receive between 30 and 100 phone calls. We will get to all of the nitty gritty in the next chapter so make sure you read it. A typical mailing campaign using our post card gets around a 3 to 5% response rate (sometimes higher and sometimes lower).

So if we receive lets say 50 calls we will typically receive 1 to 2 deals from those phone calls. Your job as a wholesaler is to sort through the calls, call back everything that looks to have good potential and put the good houses under contract.

For deal structure we typically am to make at least a $6,000 assignment fee. If we make a $6,000 fee depending on the structure we usually split the deal with the wholesaler 50/50. They get $3,000 and we get $3,000.

If we had direct mail expense of $500 from 1,000 post cards your net profit on the deal will be right around $2,500 and guess how much work you actually did?

Typically around 2 hours of work. How cool is that?

The work you personally should have done would have been setting up the marketing campaign, and sending it out (takes around 20 minutes). Then forwarding the phone calls (30 mins) and then just keeping in touch with the wholesaler to make sure he is out there putting deals together. Cha ching.

This is how you can create a 4-hour workweek life style with virtual flips.

## Closed in Sept 2014

- Sent out around 650 PostCards
- Received 30 or so phone calls
- Vacant House, Mothers old house
- Negotiated a Price of $45,000.
- Sold for $52,000
- Double closed
- My Time Invested (2 hours)
- Acquisitions manager handled everything.

**Things to Remember**
Remember to always be very skeptical when looking for wholesaler partners work with. Be slow to partner/hire and be quick to fire.

I like to put the people who I may work with through a little interview process. I want them to pretty much apply for the partnership and then I just simply ask them a series of questions and try to poke holes through their story.

Get references from them of Title companies they use, realtors, other wholesalers, and the local REIA. Make sure you call up their references and learn more about these people. Also add them on facebook and Linkedin to see what they talk about, what groups they are involved with, their pictures, etc.

Google them and find out as much about them as you can. You can even go as far as getting a background check done to see if they are legit or not. You will also want to sign a Joint Venture form with every person you partner with. The joint venture form can be found inside the Full VirtualFlips.com course.

Now the joint venture form is legal and binding but honestly it could take more money and effort to take a partner to court that its even worth if that person cuts you out of a deal. This is why sometimes controlling the property is a better solution than just giving them full control.

## How to Make more form partnerships

Because you will be getting a lot of leads coming in each and every month and typically most of the leads coming in will be sellers who want closer to retail value. These are not good deals for wholesaling but can be amazing leads for a motivated real estate agent.

What you can do with these leads is refer them off to the realtor you have choose to work with and if that realtor lists the property if you're also a licensed agent you can get a referral fee.

Typically 20 to 25%. If your not a licensed agent you can not get an actual referral fee but what you can do is have that realtor take the 20% and put it towards a marketing campaign for you. Win-Win for both of you. You will just have to have the agent check with their supervising broker to confirm how to structure this.

## Chapter end...

Remember that it may take several phone calls and weeks to find people that you actually want to work with. Do not rush into it you want to work with someone you enjoy and can have a conversation with, not someone who is trying to always 1 up you or just seems like a nut bag. Get out and make it happen.

# Notes:

# Chapter 4: How to Build the Ultimate Deal Finding Machine

"She was unstoppable not because she did not have failures or doubts, but because she continued on despite them"
**-Beau Taplin**

Now that you have a pretty good idea of how wholesaling works and the nuts and bots of the business its time to dive into the single most important factor in your success which is marketing. Marketing is what I consider to be the foundation of a good wholesaling business.

If you have a consistent stream of leads coming in each and every week you will have massive success in this business. And if you have zero leads coming in you will have zero success and pretty much quit in 2 weeks, go back to your job and be miserable for the rest of your life until it finally clicks that if I want to be free I need to get out and market the hell out of myself and dig up deals.

In this chapter we will talk about several different ways I market my business and how I have leads and deals coming to be every single day. When you are first starting out marketing is going to be difficult but believe me once you gain experience it will become easier and easier.

**The more you learn the more you EARN!**

Like I said I am a huge believer that in order to be successful with real estate investing you must become a great marketer. With wholesaling real estate you need to develop the mind and remember that you are a marketer. Your number one job needs to be to market the heck out of your self and your business. Everyone in your community needs to know that you buy houses, you pay cash and close freaky fast. The goal is to get to the point when someone thinks about selling a fixer upper the first person they think of is you. Now it's going to take time to get to this point but once you do this business gets super easy.

When I first started no one knew who I was or what I did, so I needed to educate my entire community. Now over time and sending out 2,000 plus mail pieces a month for the past 5 years people now realize what I do.   There are very few property owners in my area that have not received a mail piece from me but I still continue to market every single week and let more and more people know what I do and how I can help them.

In order to stay successful in this business you need to learn as much as possible as you can.  I am a big student of marketing and am always thinking of new and creative ways to market my business.   In order to stay ahead of your competition you need to stay on the cutting edge of what is working now.
I encourage you to study everything you can about marketing and sales copy.  Some of the best marketers to follow are Joe Vitale (get his Hypnotic writing book), Dan Kennedy (ultimate sales letter and all of his NO BS books), Ryan Deis, and Preson Ely.   Get on these peoples newsletters, buy their books and carefully watch how they market their business.

## Is Free really Free?

A lot of new and even experienced real estate investors only want to focus on ways to market their business that are FREE or nearly free.  There are several ways you can do free marketing but if you want to truly run a successful real estate wholesaling business you will need to take a risk, spend some money and market like the big boys do.

The biggest problem with free marketing is that it may take months and months to actually find motivated Sellers.  If you want to have consistent leads coming in each and every month free is not going to work for you.

Paid marketing like direct mail is a way to get your message in front of motivated sellers each and every week and it gives you a better chance of actually getting deals.

We have our marketing almost down to a science where we know that if we send out 2000 post cards to a targeted area we are going to get 1 to 2 deals out of it which profit us between $5,000 and $10,000 when wholesaling. We will dive into post cards a lot more but 2,000 post cards will cost under $1,000 to produce and could make you a quick $10,000. Not a bad return on your investment.

**Our Process!**

Before we dive into different ways to market your new wholesaling venture I want to share with you a little overview of my entire process. This is just an overview and we will break down the steps through out this chapter and others to follow.

1. Do your Market research and Find a Targeted Area to start marketing in.
2. Compile a list of Motivated Sellers (ie. Vacant houses, foreclosures, absentee owners, etc)
3. Create your marketing mail piece or set up a marketing system in this area (we will go over several ways to market your self or find deals in targeted areas)
4. Send your mail piece to the targeted area
5. Receive phone calls from people looking to sell their house & pre-screen and evaluate the leads
6. Make offers on all of the houses
7. Negotiate and put houses under contract

8. Find an Investor Buyer to assign your real estate contract to
9. Submit your deal to a title company or closing attorney (can do before step 8)
10. Close the deal
11. Collect your Check

Now that is wholesaling houses in a nutshell. You see its not a complicated process and we will cover it all inside this book. Now that you know the basics lets dive into marketing.

## Marketing for Buried Treasure

Why do I care so much about marketing and finding deals? Because if you are not marketing/finding deals, then you do not have any inventory to sell which means you do not have a business. If COKE or PEPSI did not have any pop/soda to sell would they still be in business? Of course not.

The same goes with wholesaling houses. If you do not have houses to wholesale then you will not be successful.

Before you ever do any sort of marketing you first need to know where to market to, whom to market to and how you are going to be marketing.

**This is where step # 1 comes in:  Step 1 is Market Research.**

 Inside the VirtualFLIPS.com course I teach you exactly how to go about doing your market research.  It's NOT very effective to just send out a bunch of mass marketing.  ASK me how I know this is not effective, I have tried it and lost a lot of money.

The key with market research is to find the very best cities to market in and then inside those cities FIND where cash buyers are actually buying.   There will always be 3 to 5 HOT zones in each city where you will be able to pick up deals and easily sell them with little effort.    So remember learn this step first.
Ok back to marketing and finding deals.

There are two main strategies we go about finding killer deals in any real estate market.   The first strategy consists of going after off market properties. These are houses that are NOT listed with a real estate agent.   Off market properties are by far my favorite source of deals and are what I focus on the most.   The second strategy for finding deals is going to be going after LISTED property.  These are houses listed with a real estate agent and are available to the general public.   The problem with listed properties is that because everyone knows about them there is more competition, which means it can be harder to find good solid wholesale deals.

So to start out we are going to focus on OFF market properties.

There are literally hundreds of ways to find off market properties but in this report I am going to focus on the strategy where 90% of my deals come from which is Direct mail.

**Direct Mail** is the strategy of sending out Post Cards or Letters to Potential sellers in your target area.

To get started with direct mail you first need to put a couple important pieces together. The first piece being "**WHO**" are you going to mail to. There are literally hundreds of different lists you can pull to market in a specific area. But the first list I encourage most people who are just starting out to go after is Absentee owners, and more specific, High Equity Absentee owners.

An absentee owner is someone who owns a property but has a different mailing address. This typically means they are a landlord and rent out the property or maybe they inherited the house and now its just sitting around. It could also mean they own the property but maybe moved somewhere else.

We also want to target HIGH EQUITY because we want to ensure that we mail to people that actually can sell their house for a price that we can pay. If they owe more than we can reasonable pay for a property its just NOT going to work. There needs to be equity in the deal so we can make a profit and there is enough room for another investor to make a profit also.

So what I end up doing is going to a site like Listsouce.com, FINDMotivatedSellersNow.com or RealeFlow.com to pull all of my absentee owner mailing lists. At listsource.com they will typically charge around 8 cents per name pulled (if you call and set up a corporate account, free to do). If you just set up a regular account it will be 16 cents per name. **CALL Listsouce or pay more.**

**So step 1 in pulling your mailing list will be searching their database.**

We are pulling a mailing list of High equity absentee owners. Go and Set up an account and then start your list.

ListSource™            QUICK LIST   MARKET SOLUTIONS   RESOURCES   PRICING   RESELLERS   BLOG

Dashboard

Create Your Own     Consumer Marketing     Homeowner Services     Mortgage Prospects     Investor and Foreclosure Services

Smart Marketing Starts with Smart Data                    Saved Searches/Purchased Lists
ListSource delivers the data you need to gain homeowner intelligence and
better target potential customers. With instant access to over 134 million        Recent Saved Searches

**1. Select Mortgage Prospects –Estimated Equity**

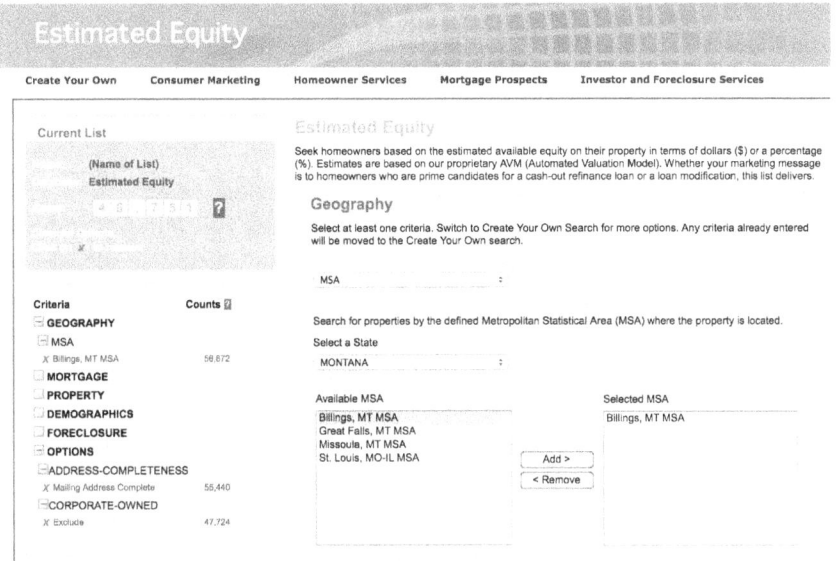

## 2. Select your MSA (city) or select specific zip codes to target

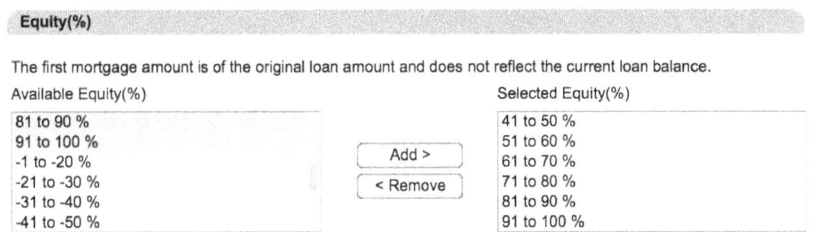

## 3. Select the Amount of equity (40 to 100%) Remember we want HIGH Equity.

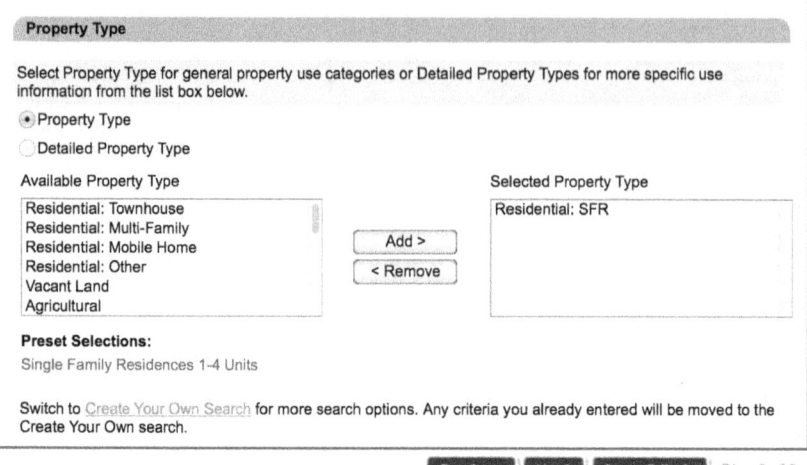

## 4. At the bottom of the Page Select Residential Single Family Residence (SFR)

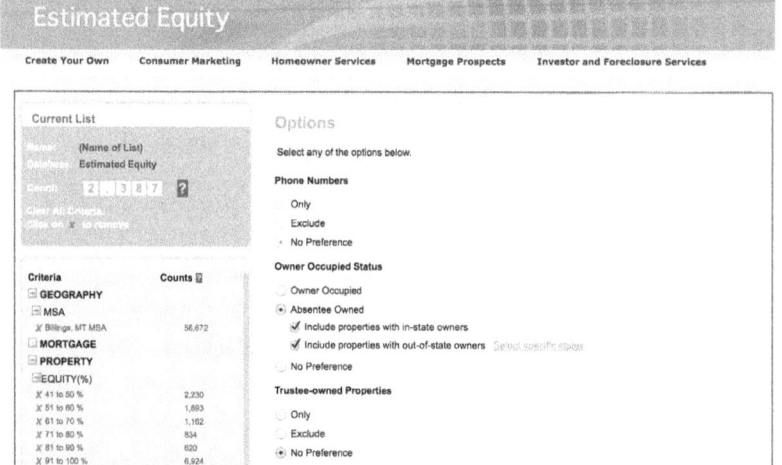

## 5. On the next page select Absentee owned.

Then you can see you have pulled a list of 2,387 High Equity absentee owners for the town of Billings MT. At this point you can pull and order your mailing list.

So once you order your mailing list it is now time to quickly sort the list in excel. What you will be doing is removing any Banks. We do not want to mail to banks, they will not respond and it is a waste of Money.

Your List will come in an excel CVS file format

## Next step....

Once we have a mailing list pulled the next thing you will wan to do is set up some kind of phone system to receive all of your incoming calls.

There are a couple different ways to go about this. You can either take all of the phone calls yourself on your cell phone (not the virtual flips way). Or you can use either a call center or use a Voice Mail System.

For my business I use a **Virtual Call Center called PatLive.com**. All of my phone calls go to the call center where the receptionist pre-screens the leads with my lead sheet (found in VirtualFlips.com) and then those leads get forwarded to me. Pat Live is not the cheapest option and is around $150 a month for 250 minutes plus $1 a minute after. So unless you are doing a lot of volume it might not be your best option.

**Patlive.com** also offers voice mail service for a lot less, which is a great option until you can afford their live receptionist.

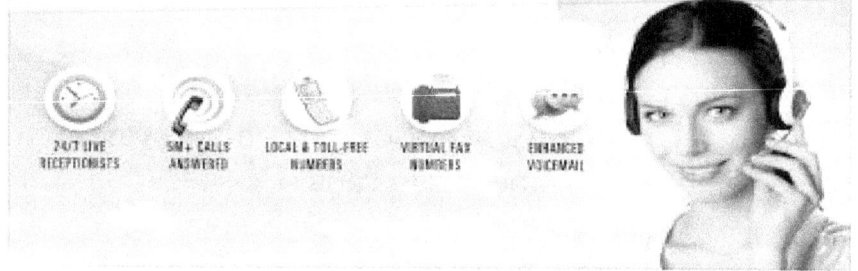

Another option for you is something like **FreedomVoice.com or ringcentral.com**. Freedom Voice and ring central are voice mail system where people call into and listen to a pre-recorded message. Then they can leave a message for you to call them back.

The Last Resort option is to use a free service like Google Voice. Google voice is simply a voice mail service provided by Google. They leave a message and you can call them back. There are lots of mixed reviews about Google voice, with dropped calls, and not receiving calls. So I recommend a paid service that is more accurate.

Remember to always call your numbers and test them out to make sure everything is working correctly. I usually like to get a different LOCAL number for each market I am wholesaling in. People seem to respond better when the number is local and not a 1800 number or out of state number.

**Setting up Your Direct Mail Campaign.**

Ok now that you have a list and a system for receiving phone calls its time to set up your marketing campaign.

There are several different types of direct mail to send out, you can do post cards, yellow letters, long sales letters, professional looking lets and more. The key is finding what works best for the types of houses you will be sending to. For us we like to focus virtual wholesaling to Working class and lower income areas. In these areas we have found post cards and yellow letters to be our preferred method.

I almost exclusively use post cards right now in my business because they are cheaper and have given me the same result as yellow letters do.

Our average response rate (number of calls) is around 3 to 5% so if we send out 1000 post cards we receive around 30 to 50 phone calls. Typically if you get 50 phone calls you should get a deal from those leads. Now yellow letters usually get a higher response rate between 5 and 10% but from our experience we typically close the same amount of deals. So you will be taking more phone calls but making the same amount of money.

I would rather take less phone calls (less expensive) and make the same amount but that is me personally. If you are already set up to maximize the potential for every lead that comes in (realtor referrals, lease option referrals, etc) then yellow letters might be a good option but if you just want to wholesale stick with post cards for now.

TO mail a post card using a site like click2mail.com who I use it typically costs around 48 cents per post card.   So if you send 1,000 it will cost you right around $480.   Yellow letters will cost in the range of $1 per letter, which will cost around $1,000 for 1,000 letters.

Ok so once you decide what type of mailing you will send to its time to set up your mailing campaign.

## Post Cards- Click2Mail.com

I have personally tested several direct mail companies and Click2mail is by far my favorite for sending out post cards.   They are the cheapest and have been the most reliable for me over the past 5 years.

# 1. Go to My Account to Get Started with Click2mail.

# 2. Select Mailing Online Classic and Mailing list

| Mailing List Name | Total | Standard | Non-Standard | International | Created |
|---|---|---|---|---|---|
| lakewood Co vacants.csv | 78 | 77 | 1 | 0 | 12/22/2014 4:22:23 PM |
| Absentee owner 59101.csv | 959 | 902 | 57 | 0 | 12/8/2014 2:22:03 PM |
| billings Dec.csv | 318 | 315 | 3 | 0 | 12/2/2014 7:55:16 AM |
| laurel Dec.csv | 41 | 41 | 0 | 0 | 12/1/2014 1:17:09 PM |
| 59101 out of state absentee.csv | 93 | 90 | 3 | 0 | 12/1/2014 12:59:19 PM |
| Great Falls High Equity Absentee.csv | 406 | 395 | 11 | 0 | 12/1/2014 12:41:21 PM |

Check All   Uncheck All                                    Refresh    Copy    Delete Checked

# 3. Upload your Mailing list and then click on the Big Click2mail logo to take you back to the home screen.   Then click on Online Classic Mail.

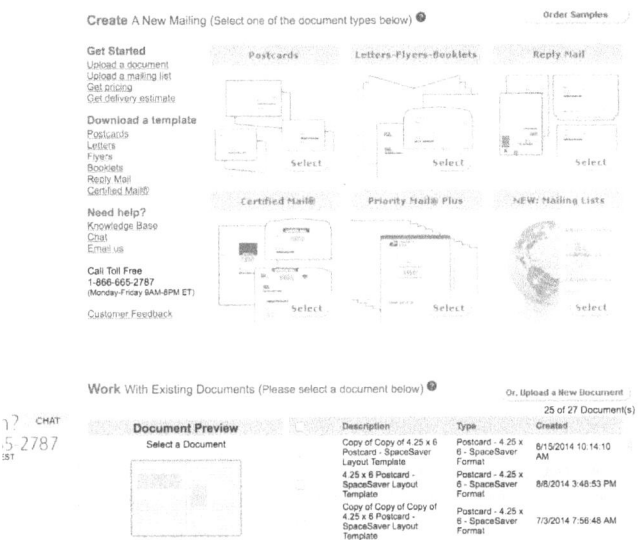

**4. Select create a NEW post card or Edit an existing document. I edit the same document each time or make a copy so I have my template already uploaded each time. This step takes me 2 minutes.**

**5. Select 4.25 Space saver layout. Your document will be blank and you will have to edit and create your new document.**

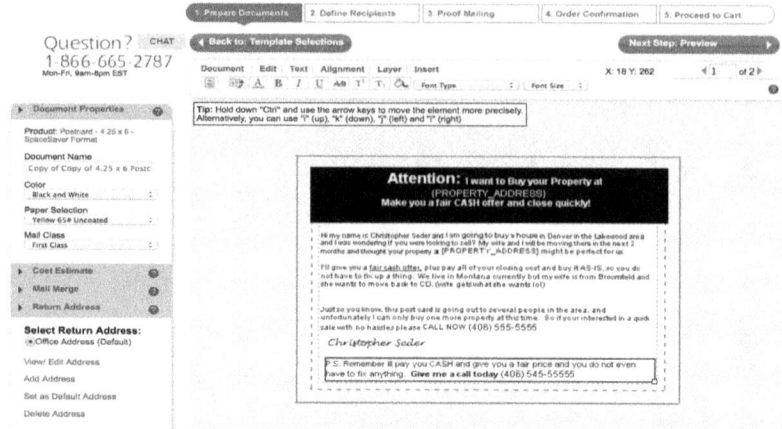

6. When editing your document you will wan to make at least 3 or 4 new text boxes. Each section of text will be a new text box. Inside the VirtualFlips.com full course there is a BONUS section explaining exactly how to set up your post card template.

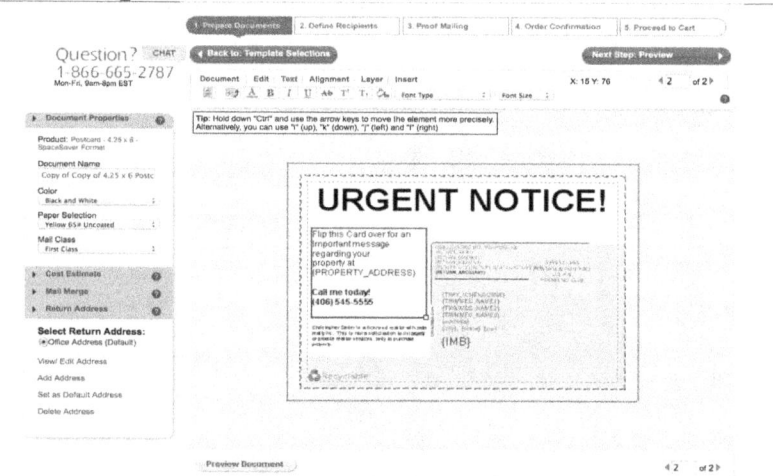

7. Remember to edit the backside of your post card. I like to use a LARGE urgent notice at the top. Then you will preview the document and make sure it looks ok.

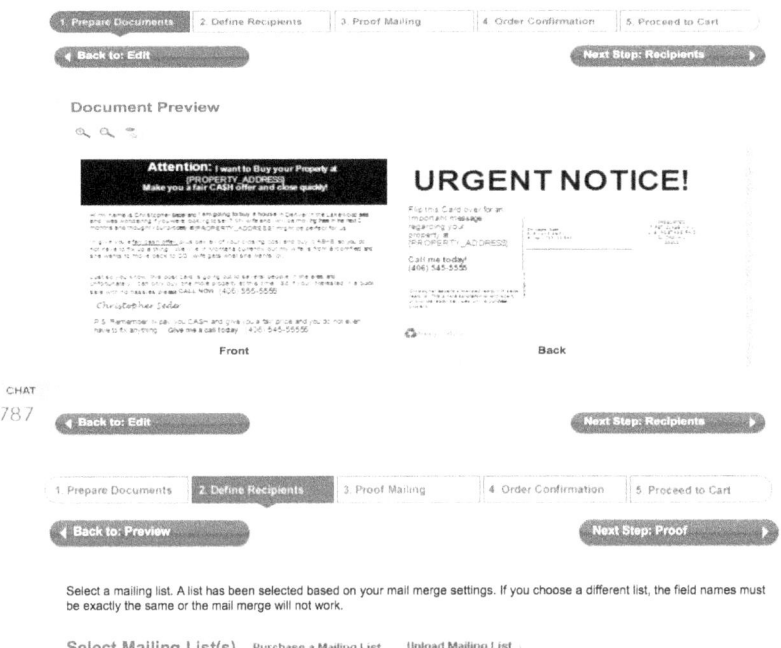

CHAT

**8. The next step you will select you're the mailing list you uploaded already.**

**Then you will be able to proof your Document to make sure everything looks correct and then you are ready to order.**

You can also use Click2Mail to send out regular letters, large post cards and a variety of other mailing pieces.   Inside the Virtual Flips Members area there is a section on HOW to create your Click2mail Campaign that is very detailed and shows you step by step.   All you have to do is watch it and follow the steps exactly.

87

## YellowLetters: GoBigYellowLetter.com

There are several great yellow letter services out there that will create and send out yellow letters for you. If you want to actually run a virtual business you cannot waste your time stuffing and stamping yellow letters yourself.

Go Big Yellow Letter offers affordable prices and has a great selection of creative yellow letters to choose from. I have used their service and they are great.

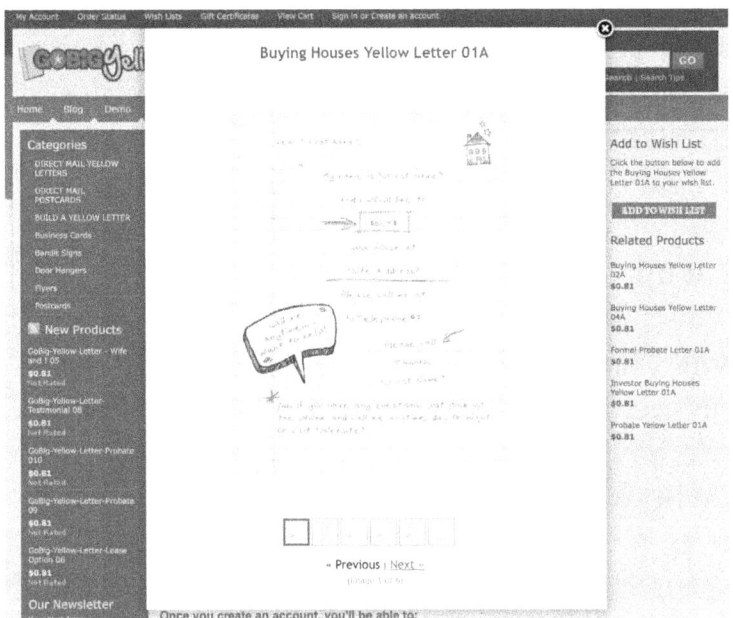

Now that you have the basics of sending out a mailing set up now let's talk about something very important before you get your mailing campaign sent out.

**In order to be successful you need to develop a marketing plan for your business.**

I have sent out 10s of thousands of post cards over the past year and come to a steady conclusion. For my business it typically takes around 2,000 post cards to get 1 to 2 deals, usually if you receive 50 phone calls you will have one good solid deal from those calls.

I know that may seem like a lot and not what most people want to hear but it's the cold hard reality of wholesaling.

You will send out 2,000 post cards costing you $1,000 and when wholesaling you typically make around $5,000 to $10,000 per deal.   So if at a min you only received 1 deal from your mailing campaign making you $10,000 you essentially made $9,000 net.   Which is not bad at all.

And the way I have my VirtualFLips.com business set up I only personally work around 2 hours on each deal but I do have assistants and acquisitions managers who work the deal.

IF I make $10,000 my acquisition manager who handles everything gets $4,000 to $5,000 and I get the $5,000 to $6,000 left over which covers my marketing expenses of $1,000 giving me a profit of $4,000 to $5,000 for only doing a few hours of work.   Not bad at all.

In this book we will not be getting into what to do once the phone calls come in, but just focusing on marketing.   A quick note is once the calls do come in then you will need to start evaluating the deals and making offers.  All of this is covered in my virtualFlips.com full course.

**Lets talk about other people to market to.**

So now you have your first mailing campaign out and mailed to, (2,000 Post cards) and you are getting lots of leads coming in and closing deals now, who else can you mail to?   Usually the first thing I do is to mail to absentee owners again but pick my either 2$^{nd}$, 3$^{rd}$, or even 4$^{th}$ best area in the town to mail to.   Once I hit that area then I start over at my TOP area with a new mailing list other than absentee owner.
**Some of my favorite lists include.**

- **High Equity Vacant Houses**

One of my very favorite sources of consistent deals is vacant house's I personally have made more money with vacant houses than any other niche around. The one big problem with doing virtual wholesaling is that you cannot actively go out and search for vacant houses in a market that is 3,000 miles away. So the very next best option is to use a service that provides vacant house lists.    The service that I use is called FINDMOTIVAEDSELLERSNOW. It is a nationwide database of vacant houses, you can mail to.   Go to http://virtualflips.com/fmsn/ to check out Find Motivated Sellers NOW.

I know what your thinking how in the world do they know if a house is vacant or not? Good question and the short answer is I don't know. They are not 100% accurate on if a house is vacant or not but in some areas they are close to 80%, which is great for us.

The software is not cheap its around $997 but that gets you lifetime access where you can pull up to 12,000 names each month. Think about it if you start sending out 1,000 to 2,000 mailing per month costing you $80 to $160 just to pull a list from listsource.com it would cost you between $960 to $1,920 per year just for your mailing lists. But if you purchase FMSN its just one time and you have all of the mailing lists you need.

- **Probate**

One of my other favorite sources of leads is Probate. Probate happens when a person passes away and the estate opens up a probate case to settle the estate. A lot of times the Heirs inherit a property that they DO NOT want or can not afford so it's a great opportunity to pick up a property for very little.

PROBATE COURT
PUBLIC FORMS

To get probate cases you can mail to you will need to either physically go down to the counties courthouse and pull records or you will need to access the counties online court records.

Call up the country and find out if they have online access to the records.   If they do not, you may need to hire someone in that market to go and pull the probate files for you.

There is also a mailing list company called USLeadList.com who can sometimes provide probate records in different areas.   Contact them to see if they have anything available in your area.

- **Pre-Foreclosures**

A pre-foreclosure is someone who is facing foreclosure but the bank has yet to take back the property.  Every state laws are different regarding the time it takes to foreclosure in my state its around 5 months for the foreclosure to be filed and 90 days to 120 days for the foreclosure sale to happen.  Or something like that.

So for those 8 months a person is late on mortgage payments is your chance to wholesale the property if the owner is motivated and wants to sell.

To find a good solid foreclosure list in your area you can contact your local counties clerk and recorder and see how you can go about getting the list. You can also contact a local title company and see if they provide a list. I get a list mailed to me monthly from a Local title company.

American Title & Escrow          Yellowstone - Montana          For More Information Call 406-248-7877

Scheduled Sales

| Notice of Default | Property Address | Sale Date and Time | Principal Balance | Original Deed of Trust |
|---|---|---|---|---|
| 3715983 Date Recorded: 08/29/2014 | 1302 PARKHILL BILLINGS, MT 59102 Loan Amount: $161,837.00 | 01/26/2015 1:00 P.M. | $156,385.33 | 3515983 |
| 3718388 Date Recorded: 09/19/2014 | 562 KILLARNEY BILLINGS, MT 59105 Loan Amount: $124,000.00 | 01/28/2015 11:00 A.M. | $116,578.91 | 3522977 |
| 3719332 Date Recorded: 09/30/2014 | 2808 S 8TH AVENUE SOUTH BILLINGS, MT 59101 Loan Amount: $9,800.00 | 01/28/2015 10:00 A.M. | $9,083.89 | 3155934 |
| 3718249 Date Recorded: 09/18/2014 | 2885 FARLEY BILLINGS, MT 591017328 Loan Amount: $1,785,291.00 | 01/29/2015 2:00 P.M. | $1,785,291.00 | 3673669 |
| 3718261 Date Recorded: 09/18/2014 | 2980 CHIEF WHITE BIRD LAUREL, MT 59044-94 .. Loan Amount: $173,500.00 | 01/30/2015 11:00 A.M. | $172,984.79 | 3415164 |
| 3718764 Date Recorded: 09/24/2014 | 3440 GRANGER AVE S BILLINGS, MT 59102 Loan Amount: $37,000.00 | 02/02/2015 11:00 A.M. | $35,419.70 | 3583337 |
| 3719134 Date Recorded: 09/26/2014 | 5406 LAZY WILLOW BILLINGS, MT 59101 Loan Amount: $214,527.00 | 02/02/2015 11:00 A.M. | $213,048.93 | 3685787 |
| 3720015 Date Recorded: 10/06/2014 | 20 IDAHO LAUREL, MT 59044 Loan Amount: $106,837.00 | 02/03/2015 1:00 P.M. | $104,373.85 | 3523071 |
| 3719658 Date Recorded: 10/02/2014 | 324 MILES BILLINGS, MT 59101 Loan Amount: $112,000.00 | 02/09/2015 11:00 A.M. | $111,224.24 | 3652162 |
| 3719810 Date Recorded: 10/03/2014 | 1128 DAYTON BILLINGS, MT 59105 Loan Amount: $145,000.00 | 02/09/2015 11:00 A.M. | $141,394.03 | 3447634 |
| 3719431 Date Recorded: 09/30/2014 | 2802 DAISY BILLINGS, MT 59105 Loan Amount: $294,462.00 | 02/10/2015 1:00 P.M. | $291,381.24 | 3513971 |
| 3720824 | 1183 MATADOR BILLINGS, MT 59105 | 02/13/2015 11:00 A.M. | $227,767.02 | 3668975 |

What I do with the list is then look up the owners names in my counties tax assessors web site and either give them a phone call (find their number) or I send them a letter.

Most people who are in pre-foreclosure wait until the last minute (right before the sale) to actually sell the house. So you may have to mail these people a couple times and call them a few times.

- **Tax Liens**

Tax Liens and Tax Sales are when someone has not paid their property taxes. The county auctions off tax liens to individuals who then purchase those taxes with the hopes of receiving either a return on their money or foreclosing on the property and taking it back at tax sale. In some states it can take up to 3 years before someone can foreclose on the property.

The good thing about tax liens is that before the house forecloses you can contact the owner directly and try and buy the property from them. This is a great way to pick up a house for a good discount as long as there is equity in the property.

To get a tax lien list you can use a service like RealeFlow.com who has lists provided with their software or you can pull them form your counties tax assessors office. My counties have the lists provided that you can download.

**Now that you have compiled a few different mailing lists remember you need to be sending out 2,000 ish mailers each month.**

Here are some things to keep in mind when marketing to off market properties.

1. Consistency: Don't just send out a few post cards 1 month and never do it again. Being consistent with marketing will make you successful.
2. Track your results: Its import to learn what is working best in different areas. Send out 1000 post cards and write down your Reponses and how many deals you received, then try out yellow letters and see if there is a difference.
3. Monitor and adjust: Overtime you will learn what is working and what is not working and you can focus 90% of your effort on what works best for you. You always want to be adjusting your strategies to what is working best NOW and learn from all of your failed campaigns.

**Your Action Steps:**
1. Compile a NEW mailing list in your target area (remember do your market research, don't go about it BLIND)
2. Set up your Voice Mail System
3. Set up a click2mail campaign
4. Wait for calls to come in
5. Repeat the process

The only way to make it happen with real estate investing is to TAKE action. You can either sit on the couch and do nothing or sit on your couch and take action.

## Seven Ways to get FREE motivated Sellers Leads

Now if your like me you sometimes fell like spending outrageous amounts of money all the time sending out mailing campaigns can get a little spendy. I like to use a mixture of paid marketing with a few cool ways to find deals that do not cost very much at all but can produce results. Sending post cards is by far my favorite and will produce consistent results but there are other ways to find decent deals.

### 1. Craigslist

Craigslist has become a great place for people to post houses they need to sell, rent, or a place for someone to find a house. Make it a habit to start farming craigslist every day or so and just browsing for houses. Every once in a while we will find a gem on craigslist. This is not going to produce 100s of high quality motivated sellers but you may pick up a few. You can also start emailing all of the FOR rent listings and see if any of these people want to sell.

You may find a motivated tired landlord or someone who has other property they want to liquidate.

**2.  Referrals from Real Estate Agents.**

Once you become established and people know what you do and know you are a legit real estate wholesaler you will start receiving referrals from others.  One of my favorite referral sources is a real estate agent.   We have had several agents contact us because they where about to list an UGLY fixer upper.  They knew we specialize in buying ugly houses AS-IS and closing on them quickly.   So before these houses where even listed they contacted us and gave us first crack at them.

Start talking with agents, look at some of the agents that are very active in listing fixer uppers, rentals and vacant houses.  These are the agents that you want to start talking to.

**3.  Search Engine Optimization**

What the heck is Search Engine Optimization (SEO). Well simply put its getting your WEB site (s) ranked on the first page of google so anyone that searches a term like "We Buy Houses Billings" finds you first. This is a great way to have motivated sellers calling you or opting in to your web site on a weekly basis.

I could write an entire book about SEO and how to get on the first page of google but there are tons of experts out there that specialize in this, so go out and find a simple ebook or blog article on this topic and read up.

One quick note, there are companies that charge hundreds of dollars each month and say they a SEO experts. MOST are scams so do not fall for them. With a little knowledge you can do it yourself.

### 4. Property Scouts

A property scout is someone is actively out looking for vacant houses for you. I have several people who are always on the hunt writing down addresses of vacant houses and sending them over to me. Start talking with friends and family members and tell them that if they find a vacant house or fixer upper to write down the address, send it over to you and if you end up purchasing the property you will pay them a $250 to $500 referral fee.

You can pay them when the house closes out of your $2,000 to $10,000 profit you make.

### 5. Video Marketing

Video has become KING of the Internet. People love watching youtube videos and sellers love seeing a face with which they will be contacting before they contact you. Set up your own youtube account and start creating little videos targeting KEY words sellers in your area might search for like "How to Sell a House", "We Buy Houses area" etc.

When a seller searches in google your video may come up on the first page. The seller than can watch the video and get into contact with you via a phone number or web site. It's a great way to start doing some SEO and also getting more exposure.

### 6. Google Business Listings

Google is by far the biggest and best search engine right now. MOST people search google first when looking for their real estate answers. You can set up a FREE google business listing for your business (search google for more info). This way when someone searches a keyword term that you have chosen your business will come up first.

### 7. Title Companies

Title companies have a vast knowledge of what is going on the real estate market, who is buying and who is selling. Get in good with a local title company and let them know that hey if you ever have a seller that seems pretty motivated and their sale falls through feel free to pass our info a long to them and let them know we are actual buyers and can maybe help them by buying their house.

This is another way that once you have built up a little credibility in your market you can start getting leads referred to you on a monthly basis.

# Other Ways to FIND off Market Properties.

There are hundreds of ways to find real estate deals some ways I find a easier than others but in order to run a successful real estate wholesaling business you should do a combination of several different marketing strategies. Then you should focus 80% of your efforts on the top 2 or 3 strategies that bring in most of your deals. The other 20% you should do but not focus a lot of effort into them.

**Driving for Vacant Houses:** As you travel around town, always keep your eyes open for distressed property. When you are heading to work or school or the grocery store start driving a few extra neighborhoods and look for vacant houses and fixer uppers.

Look for tall grass, peeling paint and sagging porches. When you see that characteristic, copy down the address so you can research the house later. I keep a note book in my car where each week I compile around 100 vacant house addresses.

Once you have a list of vacant houses the next set is going to be to look up who owns the property on your counties tax assessors web site. Start an excel spread sheet or a google drive spread sheet and put in the vacant house address, owners name, their address, city, state and zip code.

Once you have around 100 vacant houses found and looked up then you will want to take that list and upload it into click2mail and send them a post card or a letter. You can also try and call these people. Inside VirtualFLIPS.com we have a section on how to call up vacant house owners.

**Bandit Signs:** You've seen them on telephone poles, and they can generate calls. Just be mindful that some communities have an ordinance against placing such signage in public areas, and any fines may be expensive.

You can buy signs from www.ezsigns.net (800-276-3902) and from www.signwarehouse.com (800-699-5512).

Our signs say "We Buy Houses" Any Condition, Any Situation, Call xxx- xxx-xxxx Today." We always use the yellow background with black lettering.

I BUY HOUSES!
ANY CONDITION
555-555-5555
www.yourwebname.com

The signs we buy are 24"w x 18"h, and they cost about $3/ea., depending on the quantity. You'll also need to buy the wire stakes, which cost about $1.50/ea., unless you buy 500 or more.

I have also used Hand Wrote signs where I buy the sign material at wal-mart and then write on it with a LARGE sharpie. Make sure its very large lettering.

I would start with putting out 100 signs a week for 8 weeks. Some will get taken up by the local city maintenance crews. You will want to call the city's building department to see what kinds of rules they have regarding bandit signs. Don't waste money by putting signs everywhere only to have them taken down by the city, and have the city fine you for violating there rules. Do your due diligence first and call the city and ask them what their policy is.

**Internet:** This is a whole separate course, but you can use other forms of marketing to direct prospects to your Webpage. Creating the Webpage does involve some minor expense.

I use several web pages designed to help me drive traffic.

And example of one is ChristopherBuysHouses.com Most of my sites are squeeze page type web sites designed to do one thing and that is get sellers to either call me or enter their info.

**Classified Advertising:** Another great way to advertise your company is to place small classified ads online or in small local papers.

This used to be a great marketing technique for newspapers and offline magazines. Those methods are very outdated today but they can still work. I personally do not run classified advertising now because I focus on direct mail but when I did I would advertise on the front page of the Thrifty Nickel.

The first week that I posted an ad in the thrifty nickel around 4 years ago I received a deal where I made $20,000 on it.

**Example ads we use look like this:**

"Cash offer for your House today, all these other ads are jokes"
Call (406) 555-5555 for a quick cash offer.

This adds may be a little scary for you to post but it works and it is different from the rest which is important. Always be different.

**Billboards:** Expensive, but a great way to get market exposure and generate leads. Some companies, in my local area will offer Billboards for around $500 a month or less. I have a friend that owns some commercial property that was offering Billboards for around $300 per month.

For billboards and large signs use the same methods we recommend for bandit signs. A direct message with a strong call to action.

**Sell Your House Fast For Cash Any Condition, Any Situation Call xxx-xxx-xxxx today**

Or " CASH offer for your HOUSE TODAY!" No Commissions, NO Hassles, QUICK Sale.
Make sure that it stands out.

For most investors, these forms of advertising don't fit in their budget. I definitely don't recommend using this strategy unless you have the money to test it and the capacity to manage all the phone calls you'll get from the billboards. Every lead is worth something, so you have to answer the phones live when you set up these campaigns. Never ever let the calls go to voice mail. You typically have just one shot at connecting with someone over the phone. Many times a homeowner won't answer your returned call if they have to leave a voice mail.

This is why you need to set up a Call Center for this type of advertising.

**Television:** TV can give you instant credibility in your real estate market. Even a commercial can make you an overnight celebrity. A 30-second spot in your market may not be as expensive as you think because networks are looking to make up for losses in advertising. Again, this is a fantastic way to generate leads. I have a friend in my own real estate market that was paying less than $500 a month for 30-second commercials that ran on local TV channels. I cannot remember how many commercial spots he had received but it seemed like a lot for the price.

I would contact one of your local TV stations and ask them what you can do to go about creating a TV commercial.   To produce a decent TV commercial you really do not need to spend a lot of money on producing the commercial.   You can write up a script yourself (learn direct response copy writing). And you can do a power point and have someone on like Fiver.com who has a good voice do the voice over for you.

**Final Thoughts on Off Market Marketing**
Now we have covered several ways you can start marketing for sellers in any real estate market and start generating Motivated Seller leads on a weekly basis.

Remember the key is to be consistent and just get as much marketing out as you possibly can.   Right now with Virtual Flips we focus our efforts on Direct mail, which is working best for us.   They key with any marketing is just to get started and be consistent. Now lets get into finding deals with listed property.

# Finding Deals with listed Property

To be successful with wholesaling real estate you need a good combination of Off Market marketing and also making offers on listed property. We want to try and take advantage of every potential deal we can find in a given market. Right now a lot of real estate markets across the country are pretty HOT. Which means listed property inventory is DOWN and there is more completion. Now this does not mean that you will not find good solid deals on the MLS it just means it could take more offers to get 1 deal and might Listed Deals might be fewer and father in between.

I still focus on making at least 5 to 10 offers on listed property a week in each real estate market I am wholesaling in. So this needs to be your goal when going after listed property. You want to make at minimum 1 offer per day. Write that down and make it a goal. I use the saying "5 offers a week will keep the Bill collector away". We find that it usually takes us around 20 or more offers to get 1 deal.

So lets make this section quick and easy so you can get out and start finding deals and making money.

**What to do first….**

The first step before you even think about making an offer is just like marketing it's to find out the very best area in your town to start making offers.
We use Module 1 in the Virtual Flips course to determine the exact area inside a given real estate market where we will potentially have the best success.   Once you do your market research then its time to start pulling real estate listing and making offers.

**Step 1:  Have Realtor Set you up on an auto search or set yourself up**

In every real estate market I go into I have the realtor who helped me do market research set me up on an auto search campaign.    You can either have the realtor manually set you up or some realtors have what is called an IDX website where you can set up your own login and search criteria.   Then when ever a listing with the search criteria you set comes available you will receive an email.     Below is what an example email might look like and also there is an example of an IDX website.

See how the listings SAY IDX on them. This is what you want to look for when searching a realtor's web site to subscribe to.

Remax.com is a good nationwide brand that has good solid IDX web sites you can check out and get on their searches.

**Step 2: Have your Realtor pull a LIST from inside the MLS.**

Now that you are on an auto search you can sit back and wait for potential deals to be emailed to you but while your waiting you need to start making offers on houses that are already listed.

I like to really dig deep inside the MLS and pull out deals most people over look.   This is how you find Super motivated sellers inside the MLS.

What I search for is houses that have been on the market for over 90 days (longer the better), which are vacant and are possible fixer uppers.   So how to so go about doing this?

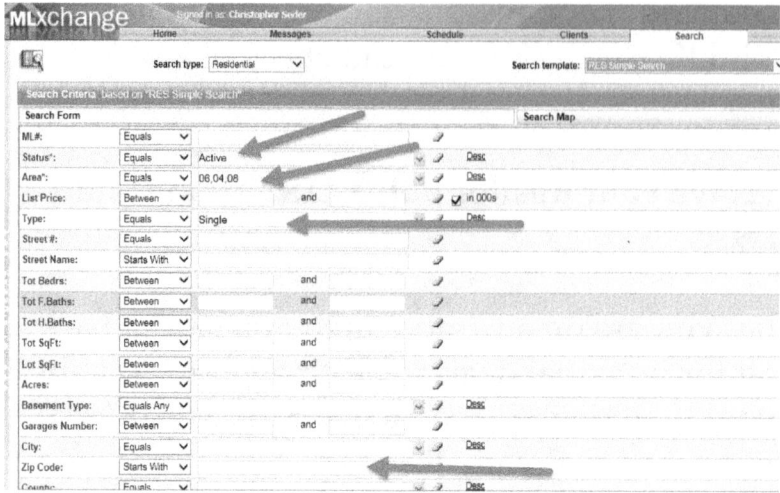

You will want to search Active Listings, Single family houses (optional: beds and bathrooms)

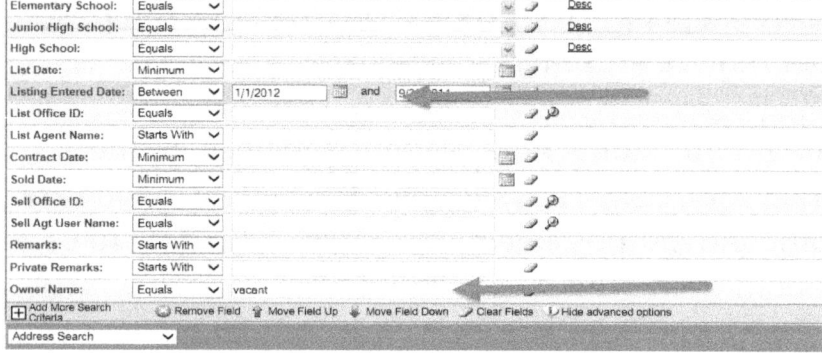

Search for listings that have been on the market for more than 90 days.

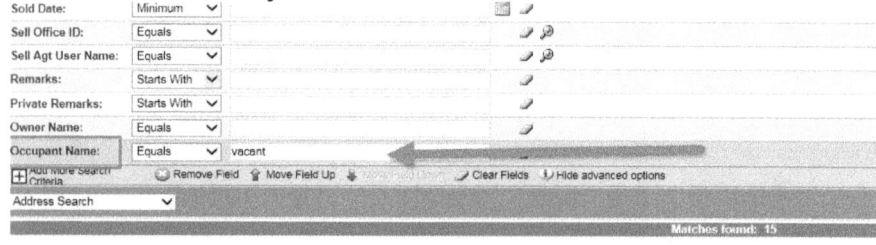

I Like to search Occupants NAME (who is living in the property and search vacant)

Then you will have your realtor send you the list of houses on the market.

Ask the realtor if he/she can provide you with the AGENT view form, that way you can see all of the comments and info only agents get to see.   There area great clues inside the private remarks.   This can be your indication if the property owner is super motivated or now.

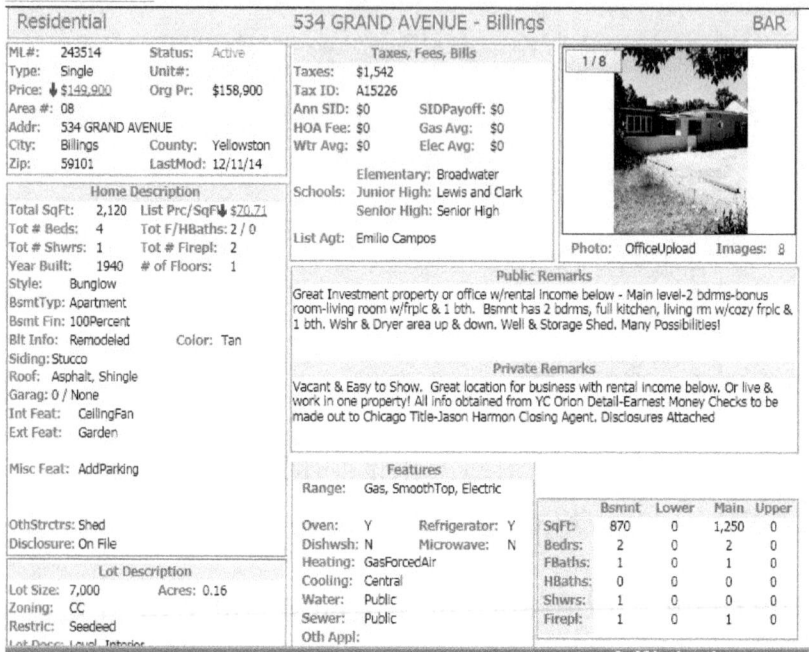

**Residential** — 534 GRAND AVENUE - Billings — BAR

ML#: 243514 | Status: Active
Type: Single | Unit#:
Price: ↓ $149,900 | Org Pr: $158,900
Area #: 08
Addr: 534 GRAND AVENUE
City: Billings | County: Yellowston
Zip: 59101 | LastMod: 12/11/14

**Home Description**
Total SqFt: 2,120 | List Prc/SqF↓ $70.71
Tot # Beds: 4 | Tot F/HBaths: 2 / 0
Tot # Shwrs: 1 | Tot # Firepl: 2
Year Built: 1940 | # of Floors: 1
Style: Bunglow
BsmtTyp: Apartment
Bsmt Fin: 100Percent
Blt Info: Remodeled | Color: Tan
Siding: Stucco
Roof: Asphalt, Shingle
Garag: 0 / None
Int Feat: CeilingFan
Ext Feat: Garden

Misc Feat: AddParking

OthStrctrs: Shed
Disclosure: On File

**Lot Description**
Lot Size: 7,000 | Acres: 0.16
Zoning: CC
Restric: Seedeed
Lot Desc: Level, Interior

**Taxes, Fees, Bills**
Taxes: $1,542
Tax ID: A15226
Ann SID: $0 | SIDPayoff: $0
HOA Fee: $0 | Gas Avg: $0
Wtr Avg: $0 | Elec Avg: $0

Elementary: Broadwater
Schools: Junior High: Lewis and Clark
Senior High: Senior High

List Agt: Emilio Campos

Photo: OfficeUpload | Images: 8

**Public Remarks**
Great Investment property or office w/rental income below - Main level-2 bdrms-bonus room-living room w/frpic & 1 bth. Bsmnt has 2 bdrms, full kitchen, living rm w/cozy frplc & 1 bth. Wshr & Dryer area up & down. Well & Storage Shed. Many Possibilities!

**Private Remarks**
Vacant & Easy to Show. Great location for business with rental income below. Or live & work in one property! All info obtained from YC Orion Detail-Earnest Money Checks to be made out to Chicago Title-Jason Harmon Closing Agent. Disclosures Attached

**Features**
Range: Gas, SmoothTop, Electric

| | | | | Bsmnt | Lower | Main | Upper |
|---|---|---|---|---|---|---|---|
| Oven: | Y | Refrigerator: Y | SqFt: | 870 | 0 | 1,250 | 0 |
| Dishwsh: | N | Microwave: N | Bedrs: | 2 | 0 | 2 | 0 |
| Heating: | GasForcedAir | | FBaths: | 1 | 0 | 1 | 0 |
| Cooling: | Central | | HBaths: | 0 | 0 | 0 | 0 |
| Water: | Public | | Shwrs: | 1 | 0 | 0 | 0 |
| Sewer: | Public | | Firepl: | 1 | 0 | 1 | 0 |
| Oth Appl: | | | | | | | |

You can also have the realtor search for keyword terms inside the public and private remarks such as, Motivated, Estate sale, fixer upper, foundation issues, wont go fha, lead paint, etc. Anything that might lead you to believe the house needs work and the seller would be motivated.

## Step 3: Pick out 5 to 10 houses from the list to make offers on.

You will want to have your realtor send you a BLANK copy of the States purchase and sale agreement. To make offers on listed property you have to use the realtor approved/state approved contract.

Fill the contract out and then submit your offer. When making offers on listed property you will also have to put up some kind of earnest money deposit. Typically its between $500 and $1,000 but in some states the Norm will be more.  Check with your realtor to find out what Sellers expect when it comes to earnest money deposits.

Remember to also run your numbers.  Run your after repair value, and put it through the standard formula (70% x arv – repairs-holding & closing cost-wholesale fee)    For more on making offers check out the virtual flips course.

**Step 4:  Wait to acceptances, rejections and counters.**

Once you make your offers they will be accepted, rejected or countered.   It typically takes us around 20 to 30 offers (sometimes more) to get an accepted offer.

Once accepted your paperwork and earnest money will be submitted to a title company or closing attorney and now your job is to find a buyer and wholesale the property.     Because this report is just on finding deals and not finding buyers that is all we have for making offers.

Some other places to look for potential listing deals are BANK web sites. One of the most common web site is HUDhomestore.com, this is where all of the HUD foreclosures houses are listed. They will also all be listed inside the MLS but if you want to just search HUD homes go to their web site. You will want to search for Investor (buyer type). Your realtor can make offers for you on hud houses, you will need to just give them your offer price and they can submit it inside for you. No paperwork needed until your offer is accepted.

**Search HUDHomestore.com**

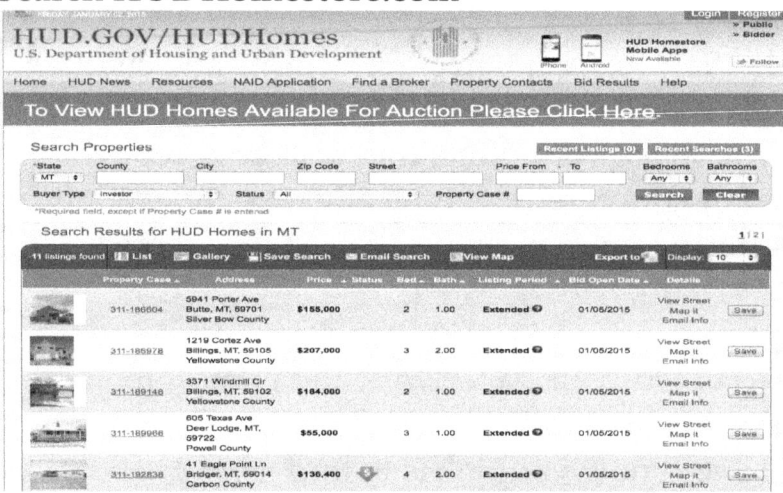

Another bank web site is HomePath.com. This is where Fannie Mae posts all of their foreclosure houses. It can be a great resource to pick up potential fixer upper deals.

## Final Thoughts...

Now that you have the basics down its time to put what you have learned into action. I want you to create a game plan for yourself and what you want to accomplish over the next 30 days.
My suggestion is that you start with Direct Mail and making offers on listed property. These are the two staples in my business that consistently produce deals.

So this week put together a mailing campaign even if it's just a couple hundred to start. JUST get started.

**If you need more extensive training remember to go to:**
http://virtualflips.com/vf-order/

Get full Virtual Flips course and learn how to take your wholesaling business to the next level.

# Notes:

# Chapter 5: Pre-screening Leads and Negotiating with sellers

"In business, you don't get what you deserve, you get what you negotiate."
*-Chester L Karrass*

"You can not reason with an unreasonable person"
-Don't remember who said

Imagine if every single day you had to answer and also return 20 to 30 phone calls. Each phone call taking between 3 to 5 minutes, what would your typical day look like? For starters you would spend at least 90 minutes to 2 ½ hours on the phone each and every day. Do you think that sounds like a fun day?

Let me ask you another question? Would you also like to spend another 2 to 3 hours each day evaluating deals, running numbers, calling people back?

All of a sudden your work day is filling up and you have not even DONE anything to work on your business all you have done is work inside the business.

For most real estate wholesalers this is the reality of their day.  They spend day after day doing the same thing over and over again.    What if I told you that I currently run my business where I maybe make and receive 2 to 4 phone calls each day?

**I don't talk to Sellers**
**I hardly ever talk to buyers (only my friends)**
**I only evaluate deals when my team needs me to**

I focus most of my time doing things that I enjoy doing in my business like writing you this sweet Virtual Flips love story (or book what ever you want to call it).    Now don't get me wrong I spent years and years slaving away taking phone calls, looking at houses, negotiating deals, etc.   These are things you MUST learn how to master but you also must learn when its time to let the rains go and find someone who can do the work for you.
In this section we are going to talk about what you need to be doing once you start getting seller phone calls coming in and also what you need to be doing to start outsourcing this entire section.

I have my pre-screening, estimating, and negation all outsourced to my acquisitions manager who handles everything. He is a stone cold killer and I could not do what I do in my business right now without him.

**Lets talk about the flow of a real estate deal.**

So at this point you should have already sent out 1,000 or 2,000 post cards and you are ready to start receiving phone calls. In the last section we talked about setting up either Pat Live or a voice mail service. If you cannot afford pat live right now that is ok but I do not recommend you use your cell phone. If you do your wife or husband is going to hate you, ask me how I know.

Ok calls are coming in, they are leaving voice mails and now it's your job to start calling these people back.

You can set aside a couple hours each day whither it be in the after noon, morning or even evening to call everyone back. What you are doing on this initial call back is simply building rapport with them and gathering info.

What I do is simply call them up "ring ring" and say, "Hello is name in? Hi my name is Christopher Seder and I received a phone call earlier regarding a post card I had sent you, is right now a good time to chat with you real quick?" They say yes. "Awesome, well I am interested in buying your property and was wondering if I could just ask you a few question about it?" Sure go ahead.

Then you go right into the lead sheet (found below) and ask them all about the property. Once you have gone through the lead sheet you simply say. Let me run some numbers on my end and come up with a fair offer and get back to you. When is a good time to give you a call back? I can call you back in 20 minutes or around the same time tomorrow if that works?

If they say 20 minutes will work, then you will need to get to work quickly evaluating the deal once you hang up. IF they say tomorrow then start calling your other sellers and evaluate that deal once you are finished with the rest.

Later in this chapter we will go though exactly how I evaluate the deal and come up with an offer price.

# How I outsource my phone calls and Never Speak to a Seller

In order for me to focus more on running my business and even helping my acquisitions manager work less I decided to use a call center called Pat Live. What they do is have a live operator who answers the phone call and then goes through a lead sheet I have pre-pared for them. The lead sheet is designed to give us some of the basic seller info we need, figure out if they are motivated and to see if it's a deal or not.

## Here is what my lead sheet looks like
### Lead Sheet

**Contact Information:**
(What's the name of the owner on title?, is there more than one person on title?)

**Phone Number:** Is the Phone number you called with the Best way to reach you?

**Email**: Do you have an email where I could send you a contract?

**Address:** What's the Address? City? Zip?

**Bed and Bath:** How many bedrooms and Bath rooms does the house have? **Square footage:** How big is the house? Square feet?

**Year Built**: What year was the house built in?

**Construction type**: Is the house a Block or Frame house?

**Property type**: Single Family? Condo, Mobile, Duplex, commercial, Etc

**Garage:** Is there a Garage?    **Any Special Features**? Pool, Hot Tub, Etc?

**Is there a Particular reason you are looking to sell?**

(I will explain the importance of this below this lead sheet, this is the most important question)

**Repairs Needed?**

What are all the repairs needed?   (Most sellers will not tell you really what needs to be done)   **I will usually estimate $15,000, until I do a full scope of work.**

**Occupancy?** Is the house currently occupied? Who? **If tenant:**  What is the Rent and when does the lease expire?

**How quickly do you need to sell?**

**What do you Currently Owe on the Property?**

(If the Seller refuses, stop and "Say Mam or Sir, I cannot make you an offer on your property unless I know this, for me to properly evaluate everything, I need to know otherwise I cannot help you)

**Are your Payments Current?   If not:  How Far behind are you?   Who is the Loan with?**

**Has a foreclosure been filed?** (Only ask if they are late on payments)

**What are you looking to get for the property?**

(If the sellers will not give you a price, simply say "Ok no problem, could you at least give me a general range of where I need to be so that I do not insult you with")

**\*\*\*If I can offer you cash and pay all your closing cost, what is the least you will accept?**

(This is the money statement, Always use this)

**Next Step.**

Once I receive the lead sheet via an email I forward the lead sheet to either my acquisitions manager or to the wholesaler/boots on the ground in a given area.

(this is a filled out pat live lead that was forwarded to my email)

At this point, my Acquisitions manager or wholesaler calls the sellers back right away if it looks like a smoking hot deal. If it seems like a marginal deal they still call them back and have a better conversation with them in order to determine if there is any profit to be made for us and to see if there is any way we can help them.

On some of the lead sheets where the seller is just way off on his numbers or what they want we do not call them back right away.

We may put them in our Freedomsoft database and call them back in a few weeks to see if anything changed. Otherwise we just do not call them.

Now some people will say you want to call everyone back which can be a good strategy but we personally get a lot of leads coming in each and every week so we do not always have the time to get back to everyone. But if we have a slow week we do make an effort to call unmotivated sellers. With the unmotivated seller leads we also just simply refer them to real estate agents who can try and list the property.

**One Key Factor you MUST determine...**
Over the years I have realized in order for you to be able to buy houses at an actual wholesale price the seller must be motivated. If a seller is not motivated there is really no reason for him/her to sell the property to you for a discount.

The 2 main reasons a person is motivated to sell at a discount is because of either some sort of financial distress or they have a property with physical distress. You need to acquire the ability to spot a motivated seller.

If a seller goes into a sob story about how they recently lost their job, or they need to pay off debt then that is usually a good indicator of motivation. You will also find someone motivated who will talk about how bad the property is or how bad his or her last renters destroyed the property. You should learn how to sympathize with them and understand their concerns.

**On to the next step…**

Once we receive the pat live lead sheet, and we determine that the deal looks to be good we either called the seller back or we just reviewed the pat live lead sheet. It's now time to run the numbers and find out if it's a deal or not a deal or if we are in the ballpark.

My focus is to go after property where the sellers and I are in the same general price range.

So to start we want to find what the After Repair Value (arv) is to determine what this property will sell for if its 100% fixed up and move in ready. What will a retail buyer pay for the property?

In order to do this we need to pull comparable sales. You can get comparable sales by having a realtor search the MLS for you and pull 3 to 5 SOLD houses that are in the general area (half mile), are similar in size, and style.

If you do not have the MLS you will want to either use a site like Zillow for quick reference or use a site like Freedomsoft, RealeFlow, or a FindCompsNOw.com to help you with the process.

What you will want to do is search a half a mile radius around the property. In freedomsoft it automatically does it for you. As you can see from the graphic above freedomsoft says this property is worth around $130,000. Which is almost 100% accurate for this property. I own a few rentals personally in this area and have done several deals there and the price they came up with is great. Now its not going to be 100% accurate for all areas but it will most likely give you a good solid starting point which is all you need right now.

So now we have come up with an ARV of $130,000 for our subject property what next?

**Note:** What the house is worth is what people are paying for the property. Not what its listed for, remember to always go off of SOLD comps. Current listings show what others are trying to sell the house for or what a realtor things they can get. SOLD comps are what matters to us.

Now its time to figure out what the repair costs for the property are?

IF you want to get a free trial of freedomsoft go to Freedomsoft-4.com.

## How to Ball Part Repair Cost

For most new real estate investors estimating repairs can be very intimidating. You thinking to yourself "I know nothing about construction how in the world do I do what it's going to take to fix up an entire house?" Some books and gurus will tell you that you MUST have a general contractor go out and give you an estimate, which if your rehabing a house is a must but for us that are wholesaling I like to take a different approach, that may shock you.
When wholesaling I use ballpark estimates. Yes I don't get exact estimates I just make educated guesses that are right 95% of the time.

The reason I do this is because I have successfully rehabbed over 50 houses in the last couple years and can tell from experience what the typical rehab project is going to cost. I know you probably don't

 have the same experience but what you can do is use my experience to estimate your repairs.

Your investor buyer will need to do his own independent inspection and determine what the repair estimates are going to be based on his own experience and his contractor. Not all contractors are going to give the same number.

I want to make sure you realize that my number is not going to be exact but it's a great starting point for initial negotiation, and coming up with your Max offer price. If you did end up estimating repairs totally wrong the good thing is in all of our offers we put in an inspection contingency. This way if you missed something catastrophic you can go back and re-negotiate the price. But we will get to that in a later chapter.

## My Estimating process:

When talking to the sellers and pre-screening them we always ask them what repairs are needed. Most sellers will tell you exactly what needs to be done or what they think but some will straight up lie to you about the condition. That's ok your boots on the ground will end up going and verifying and getting pictures so you can make a more educated guess.

First No matter what a seller says to you, even if they say the property needs zero work and is move in ready I personally still estimate a Min or $15,000 in repairs. That has become my baseline for rehabbing. I have personally never purchased a property that does not need less than 10k in repairs or have I ever wholesaled one. So My first estimate is always right around $15,000, this is because most investors if they purchase it will want to paint, do new flooring, and minor upgrades depending on what they will be doing. If it's a rental they will do the least amount of work possible, if it's a rehab they will do more.

**Here is what I usually Estimate:**  Estimate is based on a 3 bed 2 bath around 1500 sq ft house.

Seller says the property needs no work and is move in ready = $10,000 to $15,000

Seller says the property needs minor updates, paint carpet, etc = $15,000 to $20,000

Seller says property needs a lot of updating, paint, carpet, flooring, cabinets etc = $20,000 to $30,000

Seller says the property needs a lot of work  = $30,000 to $40,000

Seller says the property needs to be town down = Estimate between $50,000 and $80,000

I have done a full GUT remodel on a 1500 sq ft 3 bed 2 bath house, siding, all new sheet rock and everything it cost me right around $78,000 for the total remodel.   So that is why I base my high repairs off of.   Depending on the area and contractor it could be more.

Also remember that larger houses 2,000 sq ft will take more to rehab so add an extra 25% or so on to the rehab cost.

Do not get too hung up on figuring out repair estimates for wholesaling purposes.

You can also use the formula $20 to $25 per sq ft to estimate repairs. For a 1500 sq ft house that would be around $30,000 to $38,000 for a full remodel.

Now just for reference if you want to learn how to estimate repairs exactly the best thing you can do is go look at an actual fixer upper house, get 3 to 5 contracts to come and all give you bids on the properties broken down into exact prices for each part of the job and then use their estimate as a template for future references.

This is by far the BEST and most accurate way to go about it but because we are wholesaling virtually we do not need to be 100% accurate, but we do need to be in the ballpark. If you are not in the same ballpark you will really start to lose credibility with your buyers and also could harm your reputation by always having to cancel contracts or renegotiate.

If you're ever in doubt about what the repairs might cost always fair on the higher side.

Ok now that we have our After Repair Value and our Repairs lets start putting all of the pieces together.

**Your offer price**

The standard formula we use to determine what our max offer should be is 70% X ARV (-repairs-holding and closing cost –wholesale fee) =Max Offer

So if we look at a house that has an arv of $130,00 and we times it by 70% we get $91,000.

Then we take that $91,000 –Repairs $20,000 (estimating minor fix up) we come to $71,000

Next we want to subtract the holding cost and closing cost. Typical holding cost for an investor will be around 12% of the purchase and repairs annual interest and they usually only hold them for around 6 months if fixing and reselling. When doing this virtually I typically just factor in 10% of the $91,000. That way it makes everything easier. So 10% of 91,000 is $9,100

Take the $71,000 -$9,100 so now you are at $61,900. Next subtract your wholesale fee. You want to make between $5,000 and $10,000 so subtract $10,000, which will give you a purchase price of **$51,900.**

That is what your offer should be.

I know some wholesaler who will make offers higher than that or just make offers around 50% of the ARV and call it good.   If you where to offer 50% your max offer would be $65,000 which you could possibly wholesale the property for $70,000 and sill leave a rehabber with around $20,000 after everything.

Because I rehab a lot of houses I really try my best to make sure there is a big enough profit spread for a rehabber to be happy.

**Another way to factor MAX offer**

Another way I factor my max offer is by taking the ARV –Profit- Repairs -10% of arv –wholesale fee.

With this factor you take your $130,000 -$30,000 - $20,000 -$13,000 -$10,000 = $57,000 would be your max offer.   With this formula you are giving your Rehabber a nice 30k profit.

The best way to come up with your max offer is to talk with other rehabbers in the area to determine what they are paying for houses and what formula they use.  That way you can just decide that you need to be around $10,000 lower than their max to wholesale houses.

There is really NO right answer or exact way to do this it really depends on what investors want to make and what others expect in that particular area. In my area rehabbers want to make around $30,000 in profit when everything is done. I know in some areas rehabbers are more than happy to make around $20,000 and in others they want to make $50,000.

**Another Way to Find the Value (cool technique)**
One way that you can determine what you want to pay for wholesale property is to look at what the actual cash sales for that area where. You can determine what the average price per sq ft house in a certain area are selling for and then determine what you can offer based on that. So if you have property that is 1,000 sq ft and you know investors are paying around 63.12 for 1,000 sq ft houses you can reasonably assume that an investor could pay around $63,000 for the property. Subtract a little for repairs and your wholesale fee and BOOM you have your magic number.

+ Tulsa | View Dashboard | Analyze Properties

| Sold Property Data | View Maps | View Graphs | Sold PSF By Zip code |

Add PSF

View

Show 10 entries                                    Search: 74006

| Zipcode | Beds | Baths | PSF Avg | User Override | Actions |
| --- | --- | --- | --- | --- | --- |
| 74006 | 2 | 1 | 66.55 | | Edit | Save | Delete |
| 74006 | 3 | 1 | 35.26 | | Edit | Save | Delete |
| 74006 | 3 | 2 | 63.12 | | Edit | Save | Delete |
| 74006 | 4 | 2 | 56.68 | | Edit | Save | Delete |

## How to Map Property

What I like to do in each market is map out all of the cash sales I received from the realtor.   I upload the results into https://Mapsengine.google.com/map and then what it does in put all of the listings for you on a map.   Then when you have a property you need to comp you can search the address in the search box and see what actual cash buyers in that area are paying.

Once you know the actual amounts someone is paying you can then just take your wholesale fee off the top of that and you have your purchase price. You do not have to rely on knowing the repairs or even worrying about anything else.

For example if you see most of the sales in the area are 3 bed 2 baths houses selling for cash for $40,000, you can safely assume that if you put it under contract for $30,000 you could easily wholesale it to one of the cash investors in the area for $35,000 to $40,000.

**How to calculate what a Landlord will pay**
In some areas you will be focusing on wholesaling houses to land lords. Landlords determine what they will pay usually based on Cash on Cash return or something similar. All they really care about is how much of a return they will be getting on their money and do not care as much about after repair value.

I typically think of landlord houses as houses that are under $90,000 in ARV. This is because from my experience rehabbers want to have an arv over $100,000 in order to make a good solid spread. Once you get under the $100,000 price point your profit potential gets lower.

**Cash on Cash return** = Annual Dollar Income/Total Dollar Invested

Your annual dollar income is calculated by taking the Gross Annual Rent –Mortgage payment, repairs, insurance, management, vacancy and another other expenses. That gives you your net annual income. To get your total dollar invested you take the Purchase price (if cash) plus any initial repair cost invested.

So if you have a house where your investor purchases it for $30,000 plus there is $10,000 in repairs and $2,000 in closing cost his total investment would be $42,000. If the property rents for say $900 per month and you have $400 per month in expenses your NET income would be $500 per month or $6,000 per year. So the cash on cash return would be 14.29%. Not to bad for a rental.

To come up with what landlords would want for a purchase price you can work the formula back words. For example if someone wants a 12% cash on cash return you will know that you need to find a property that grosses at least $6,000 per year at a purchase price of $50,000. $6,000/12% =$50,000

**What's next?**

Ok so now we have learned all about how to come up with your offer price. In the next chapter we will dive into what to do next. How you can start making offers, calling back sellers and all the nitty gritty of that.

## What to remember...

Remember do not over complicate the process; it does not have to be over complicated. Use your best judgment when determining ARV and repairs. You do not have to be exact but just need to be somewhat close.

## NOTES:

# Chapter 6: You Either Make offers or Die!

"You miss 100% of the shots you don't take."
–Wayne Gretzky

**5 offers a Day keep the Bill Collectors away.**

The reason making offers has an entire chapter dedicated to its self is because I feel that this is the most important part of your real estate wholesaling business.

You MUST put all of the other pieces together but your efforts will be useless if you are not consistently making offers each and every week. The only way to officially get a house under contract so you can wholesale it is to make an offer.

If your running a virtual flips business you will want to know this process like the back of your hand so you can easily train an acquisitions manager to make offers for you or so you know the wholesaler you are working with is doing the process correctly. When making offers we structure it 2 different ways. The first way is that My acquisitions manager and I make the offer and send the contract and the wholesaler takes it from there or in some cases we structure it where the wholesaler makes the offer and puts it under contract. Whichever way you feel most comfortable with is the way you should go about doing it.

So before you make any offer you should have already went through chapter 5 and determined what the MAX you can pay for the property. Now that you have done that your next step is to give the seller a call back and make them an initial verbal offer. I personally DO NOT go an look a house unless I know that the seller and I are in the same ball park on price. Believe me when I tell you that you will waste hours and hours if you just go out look at every house, then make your offers and come to find out the seller wants $50,000 more than you could even pay. This is why I make all of my initial offers over the phone.

## Your Phone Offer

To make an offer over the phone is very simple.  All you have to do is call the seller back and say "Hey John I had a chance to run some numbers and based on the current market value, and what other cash investor's like my self are paying in the area I can offer you around XXXXX amount" Now is that something that you can work with?"

As you can see from this statement we are giving them a ballpark range and saying around XXX amount.  We will also have to make it clear to the seller if that is a price range that is acceptable to them that we will have to look at the property first to make sure there is nothing major that we over looked and also tell them that if the property is in worse condition then we thought our offer may go down but the good news also is that if the property is in better condition the offer could also go up.

And that is it.   The seller will have around 3 responses to that statement.  The first one and the one I like the best is they will say "Yes I think that is a fair price for the property."

The may also say "That is way less than I can sell the house for" (or cuss you out and hand up on you) or they will say "You know I was really hopping to get closer to XXX amount for the property is there anyway you can come up a little bit?"

If they say the latter then its time to start doing a little negotiation and see if you can find some sort of common ground with them.   Later in this chapter I will cover some negotiation tips and tricks you can use to have more success talk to sellers.    But for now lets dive into what to do next once your offer price is accepted.

When someone excepts your verbal offer now its time to set up a meeting for either you, your acquisitions manager or wholesale to go and look at the property and bring a Purchase and Sale agreement for them to sign.

**Time to Go look at the property....**

I always bring a filled out real estate contract when meeting with the seller, the agreement has all of my info filled out, and has everything down except for the sellers signature, purchase price and closing data. That way it's all ready to sign when either I get to the property or my boots on the ground gets to the property.

At the end of this chapter there will be a section on how to fill out a contract.

**What to do when you go look at a property?**

When you go and actually look at a house or have your acquisitions manager or wholesaler look at a property always make sure you are on time or a little early. Make sure that you are presentable when going there. You don't have to dress up but wear nice jeans or nice pants, and a nice polo shirt or button up shirt. You want to come off as someone who has them selves put together.

Make sure that when you are at the property to build rapport with the seller. Ask them questions; ask them about their day, etc. DO not talk to much about yourself or be too quite but just be pleasant and have a smile on your face.

I also do not suggest you bad mouth their property in front of them. Just have them give you a tour and note everything you see in a note book and make sure there is not anything that looks to be crazy that you did not factor in.

Once you are done walking through the property simply start talking to the seller about the price. Tell them you know based on the condition of the property and what we discussed over the phone I can pay right around $XXXXX amount is that something that you can work with?

If they say yes then pull out your real estate contract, fill out the purchase price and then hand them the contract and let them read over it. Answer any of their questions they have and if they are happen with it get a signature.

You will also want to make sure they are OK with you putting a lock box on the property (best to do this over the phone before you lock it up), just explain to them you want to get your contractor, and business partners over there asap to take a look at it and want to make sure they have access to it. Give them the code combination for the lock box and assure them that no one will be at the property without you (you the buyer).

## What if there is a repair that looks bad you did not factor?

If you come across something that just looks strange like a huge foundation crack or something just odd then do not rush into signing a contract or just add in another $10,000 or so onto your Rehab number (subtract from your offer).

Now if you and the seller could not agree on price right then and there what you can do is tell them you will run your numbers again and see if you can come up any higher and if you can you will shoot them over a contract.    Also if you need an inspection checklist feel free to go to VirtualFlips.com/blog and you can find a post with a free inspection checklist on it.

## Make Follow up offers
So what I do on every house that I talked to the seller or went and looked at the property but we could not agree on price is still send them an offer.   I do this by putting together a small seller package and sending it to them in the mail.

The package includes a 1-page sheet about me and my company and a 1 page sheet about the benefits of working with an investor like myself. Then it includes a real estate purchase and sale agreement with my MAX offer. I give them 3 to 5 days to get back to me with an answer or my offer is no longer available. This gives the sellers a little bit of time pressure to make a decision.

You will also want to do this same strategy with all of your 30 day or older seller leads that you where close on numbers but just could not make the deal work. Maybe you had already sent them an offer and they said no but what I like to do is either follow up with them in a month or two and give them a call and see if they are any closer to selling. You can also just send them a follow up letter and contract and see if they respond back.

---

## Simple ways to negotiate with sellers

In order to put together Killer Real Estate deals you need to become a master negotiator. Over the years and through talking to 1000's of sellers I have developed several quick negotiating scripts and one liner's that have helped me negotiate and build rapport with sellers.

One of the things that I have learned from my father is how to talk to sellers and through that I have been able to make nothing deals into deals. I have been able to buy houses from people that would not sell to anyone else.    One of the keys to my negotiation strategy with all sellers is to find out what they need and try to figure out a way to help them out.

A big thing for a lot of sellers we work with is they need to sell their house and then have enough money to find an apartment, and have moving money.   So we want to focus our negotiation on helping get them what they want.   You must understand the seller's reason for selling in order to fix their problem.   Most sellers will pretty much tell you their life story when you talk to them and will tell you exactly what they want if you just ask.

When I first got started I was DEAD scared to talk to sellers. It's intimidating when you first get started but you must realize that you need to start pushing yourself outside of your comfort zone. Getting out of your comfort zone will make you a better person and real estate investor.

We want to educate the seller as far as what is going on in the market and justify whey we offer what we offer.

## Building Rapport

In order for a seller to sell you a property at a HUGE discount they first need to like you and trust you. Our lead sheet that we provide you with it designed to help you build rapport by asking sellers questions and interaction with them.

Some sellers you will seem to have instant rapport with and others it might take a few phone calls to build that rapport.

The key to getting people to like you and to build rapport with them is to get them to feel like you are just a normal person like them. People seem to like and trust people that are similar to them. They like people that act the way they do and people that talk the way they do. A great way to build rapport is to talk like your seller.

If you have a seller that talks slow, make sure you keep your speech at the same pace as them. This goes to fast talkers too. This will help you build rapport quickly and will make negotiating with the

sellers a lot easier.

## Quick Tips

The Number one rule in negotiating is to never be the first person to name a price or He who names price first loses. Remember this rule whenever talking to a seller about buying their property. A lot of sellers will dance around the price questions and want you to just make them an offer.

**If they will not give you a number then say something like:**
*"In order for me to not waste your time I need to know that we are in the same ball park on price"*

*"In order for me to properly evaluate and give you a fair price I need to know that we are in the same ball park"*

*"Can you give me a price range that you need to be in, that way I don't bring you an offer that would insult you"*

Sometimes when you are asking a seller what price they are wanting for the property they will say something like "Well I don't want to give my house away"

You Say "I don't want you to give your house away either. But what would you feel like price range wise would be giving your house away?"

After you ask a question, always shut up. Let them blurt out whatever is on their mind. Sometimes when you just shut up the sellers will pretty much negotiate with themselves. I have had sellers say they want 100,000 for a property and all I said was something like "hmm ok" and they all of a sudden say but I might take 80,000 for it. If I would have started talking they would have never said they would take 80,000.

Another quick tip is that you should never be afraid to walk away from a deal. Remember there are hundreds of deals out there waiting for you to flip.

**How to Get People to like you!**
One of the keys we have found to negotiating is having rapport with the sellers. Building rapport is simply just finding a common ground that you can communicate with that makes people feel comfortable with you, and makes people like and trust you.

One of the fastest ways to build rapport with a seller is by positioning yourself to be like them. What I mean is that we like people that are similar to us. We like people that talk like us, people that act like us and people that have the same beliefs as us.

If you are talking to an elderly lady that speaks slowly, you need to then slow down your speech and talk like them. A person that talks slow will have a hard time relating and liking a slick fast talker.

You are there to help them out. When you put the seller's needs first you will instantly build rapport. When a seller sees that you are trying to solve their problem they will want to sell to you.

## Negotiating Price

Price will most likely determine if you are able to purchase a property or not. In real estate investing you need to be able to buy a property at a discounted price in order to make money. There are strategies that allow you to over pay and still make a profit but if you are rehabbing, or wholesaling you must buy at a discount.

Below are several negotiating phrases that we use when negotiating with sellers. These phrases help us to get home owners to drop their prices and pay what we want.

*"Why Would I buy your property when I can go around the corner and buy your neighbor's property for half the price"*

*"We talk to hundreds of people a week, and in order for us to purchase your property you need to be competitive on price"*

*"I just purchased a Similar house not too far away from here for $XXX"*

*"So if you're telling me that if I come to your house with a brief case with $100,000 cash in it you're going to tell me no?"*

## The Facts Man

Sometimes you will come across a seller who is all about the numbers. You will need to justify your price with facts like other fixer upper houses that have sold and repair cost estimates. These types of sellers will need to be able to rationalize the fact that they will be selling a property at a discount.

Whenever you pull comps there will usually be a few low sales, these are usually other fixer uppers that have sold. All you need to do is show your seller the facts and they will be more willing to negotiate price.

## How to Re-Negotiate a Deal

Sometimes you will put a property under contract at a price that might just be too high and you will have to go back to the seller and either cancels the contract or you can do what I do. I renegotiate the sales price. Currently I have almost a 100% success rate at going back to the sellers and getting them to drop their prices by 5,000, 10,000 or more.

The first thing you must always have in your contract is some sort of out clause, such as "this contract is contingent upon property passing business partner's inspection"

*"Hello, Well I have gone and talked with my business partner and I have not been able to get him to agree with us on the numbers. The price makes sense to me but I am not the only decision-maker. My funding partner must approve the deal. If he does not think the numbers make since at (price), then the funding is obviously not there. I know this is not what we talked about and I am sorry for that, but my hands are tied. Here is what we can do (price)...Is that something that will work for you?"*

Use the line above to re-negotiate price and it will work most of the time. They will see you as the good guy and your partner as the "Bad Cop".

## Negotiating Books

There are hundreds of Great negotiating books on the market today. I have listed a couple Books that I have personally read that have helped me. Remember to keep on learning and growing.

- **Influence, the Psychology of Persuasion** by Robert Cialdini
- **Pitch anything** by Oren Klaff
- **Weekend Millionaire Negotiation Tips** (book is good, do not buy anything else from them, very dated)
- **Winning through Intimidation** by Robert Ringer

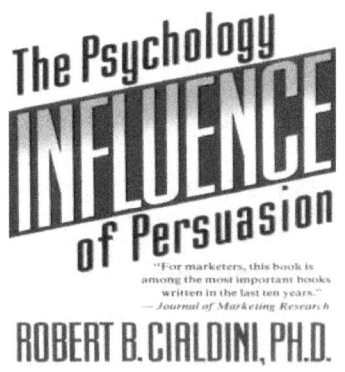

Negotiation is one of the keys to buying real estate at a discounted price.  In order to be able to get a good deal you must first position yourself in front of motivated sellers and then know how to speak to them.  If you are inexperienced or have never talked with a seller before that's ok.  I suggest you start practicing by simply calling up as many For Sale By Owner Sellers as possible.

The more people you talk to the easier it will get before soon it becomes like second nature.  You are going to make mistakes and mess up.  I have messed up 100's of times talking to sellers but I have learned from my mistakes (many times) and every conversation has made me a stronger negotiator.

**Key things to remember when making offers**

The number one key you can remember when making an offer is that if you are not somewhat ashamed of your Offer then your offer is TOO high. We are not scum bags trying to low ball people we are just trying to solve the sellers problem my offering them a price that 90% of other real estate investors are willing to pay.

And remember to make an offer on EVERYTHING, it's a numbers game and the more offers you make the more success you will have.

# How to fill out a Contract

If you have never filled out a real estate contract you are probably imagining it as being harder to do than nuclear physics. But filling out a contract really is not that difficult and the contract I use for OFF market properties is only 2 pages long. If your making offers on listed property you will want to get a copy of the State Real Estate Contract from a local realtor and the best thing to do is sit down with one of them and have them step you through how to fill it out. You can then have them write you and example contract that you can keep on file for reference.

Ok to start with a contract lets look at a picture of one.

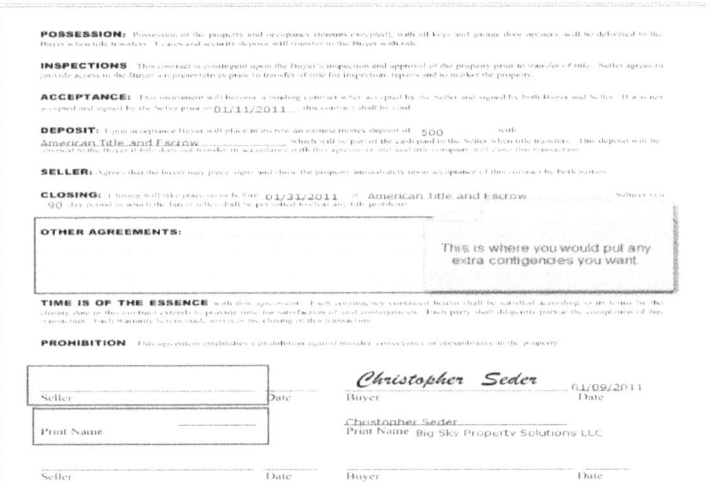

As you can see from this contract (some of it is cut out) there is really not a ton of things for you to add. You will want to make sure you have:

- Buyers Name (and or assign)
- Sellers Name or Owner of Record (sellers name also on the bottom)
- Inspection period (15 days to 20 days)
- Legal Description (found on county tax assessors site)
- Address
- Earnest money deposit ($100 to $500)
- Close Date (normally 30 days)
- Title Company
- Signatures (include address's and phone numbers)
- Contingencies

And that is really all you need to fill in.

Some of the contingencies we include are:

- Contingent on property inspection and approval of partner
- Subject to a Home inspection
- Buyer is a real estate investor who buys and sells for profit
- Purchaser requests permission to have access to the property upon signing of contract, to show prospective contractors, home inspectors, business partners, and investors.
- The buyer may assign his contract to another company or real estate investor who will close on the property
- Buyer is a licensed relator with _____realty in the state of MT (if you're a realtor)
- Buyers liability is limited to his earnest money deposit

If you would like more info on filling out a contract go to http://VirtualFlips.com and get the full course, we have video tutorials inside the members area that will provide you with everything you need.

## How to make an offer on a Listed Property

Now we have covered how you should make offers on unlisted property by simply using a 2-page contract.   In this quick section I want to discuses some basics of making offers on listed property. These will be houses listed on the MLS.

When making an offer on a listed property you will not be directly negotiating with a seller, you will have to make an offer through their listing agent or through your own buyers agent and then he makes the offer to the listing agent.   Now the one big problem with making offers like this is that it's hard for you to build any rapport with the seller.  All you can really do is offer them a cash price with a somewhat quick close.

The first step in making is listed offer is to put together your template purchase and sale agreement. To do this I recommend you sit down with a real estate agent and have them help you fill it out.  Most State Real Estate Contracts are over 8 pages long and have a ton of info in it.   But really all you need to do is get your BASE info filled out to start, like your name, company, contingencies, etc.

You will pretty much use the same contingencies are you do with unlisted property. The one thing that may change is if you are making offers on Bank Owned property. Then you will have to use their contracts and their contingencies. I know it's a pain but it has to be done.

Once you put your offer together all you simply have to do is have the realtor send out your contract and BOOM you are all done. All you have to do is wait for them to reply with a counter, a rejection or an acceptance.

If they accept your offer you will want to get your earnest money to the title company and have them start the closing process. Boom you are all done and then you just have to wholesale the house.

**MLS offer Case study…**

I want to tell you a quick story about an MLS deal I did not to long ago. The reason I am telling you this is because it's proof that you can find hidden gems inside the MLS. OK so one day I decided to pull all of the houses listed for sale in the MLS over 90 days that had "fixer upper" inside the remarks.

I came across one deal that looked to be promising. It ended up being a 3 bed 1 bath, house with one crappy picture of the exterior, which as beat up.

The property was currently rented and needed 48 hours to look at the property.  (if its harder to see the inside its less likely other will put in the effort).  The house was listed right at $59,000, which I thought was more close to retail for houses in that area.  I decided I would take a shot and my initial offer was $22,500.  Way below what it was listed for.

Low and behold the sellers countered me at $35,000 and I countered back at $27,000 and we met at $29,000.  And I did not even look at the property. So after the house was under contract I set up a showing to go look at the property and on my way to look I decided to call one of my good friends who is a cash buyer and see if he might be interested.

He was more than ecstatic and met me at the property.  We both where amazed at how nice the inside of the house was.  Right then and there the buyer said he would pay $35,000 for the property and I assigned him the contract that day for $6,000 spread.

In less than 2 weeks he closed on the house and I had a $6,000 check in my hand.

The lesson here is that you should just start making offers because you never know what you're going to get.

## Chapter Conclusion...

As you can see from this nice long chapter there is a lot that goes into making an offer and its so very important that you develop a system where you are making offers on everything that might be a potential deal.   The more offers you make the better you will be off in the long run.

From experience the people who I see succeed with real estate wholesaling are the ones you make a crap load of offers, I mean a lot and the people who do not succeed are the ones that maybe make 2 or 3 offers here and there and then wonder why they never make any money.

So get out and make a ton offers.

# Chapter 7: Where are all of the Cash Buyers Hiding?

"Number one, Cash is King...Number Two Communicate...Number Three, Buy or Bury the Competition."
**-Jack Welch**

To complete a successful wholesale deal you first need a motivated seller and then next you need a buyer. I like to work with either cash buyer or a financed buyer that can close fast.

Because we will be doing our deals virtually and working with an experienced wholesaler finding buyers will usually not be your responsibility. But sometimes you will come across a property and your wholesaler just can't seem to find a buyer for the thing. So this is why you need to know the basics of building a buyers list and learn some easy steps to follow.

I personally have built a large buyers list of a few hundred people in my area but I still wholesale 95% of my deals to my main 5 cash buyers, That's right you do not need a large buyers list all you need to really know is who are the actual legit cash buyers who can close fast and who are buying a lot.

Its like of like the 80/20 rule. Which states that 80% of your deals will be sold to 20% of the people on your buyers list. In my case it's more like the 95/5 rule.

So your main goal needs to be to build up a large buyers list but focus on finding the 5 to 10 buyers who will be the easiest to work with and make decision fast. Then those people will be your VIP buyers who you will call first whenever you get a deal.

**QUICK NOTE:** Worry about putting deals together before you think about building a buyers list. If you have deals buyers will be easy to find.

Just my philosophy.

Ok so here is my quick process for wholesaling a house. We will dive into building your buyers list and more ways to find buyers in the next few pages. So this little section starts off after you have signed a contract with the seller.

## Put the Property under contract

- o Negotiate the purchase price and terms of contract
- o Select Closing Date 14 to 30 days
- o Get Keys or Put lockbox on the property for access
- o Get 4 to 8 exterior pictures, and picture of each room of house
- o Pictures of any damages
- 3 days after Take the Contract and earnest money to the title company
  - o Have the title company start the title work
- The Day of signing the real estate contract put together marketing piece to send to buyers
  - o Brief description of Property (be creative)
  - o After Repair Value -3 comps to support price
  - o Repair Estimate
  - o For Rental: Average rents in area
    - ▪ Normal expenses (taxes, utilities estimate, mortgage etc)
    - ▪ Property Management fee and company referral
  - o Photos of the Property
  - o Affiliate link for book or course (multiple streams of income)
- Upload property, Photos and description to freedomsoft or RealeFlow
  - o Syndicate property
- Call up top 5 Buyers and email them the property
  - o Give them 1 hour to decide then move onto next buyer
- Send Email to Buyers List
- Set up Showings to view the property

- Day 3 Pull all of the recent cash sales
  - MLS cash sales
  - Find Cash Buyers Now
  - Look up the owners of recent cash sales and skip trace them and call them.
  - Add everyone to your buyers list
- Day 3 Post craigslist ad
  - Be creative, No address, send buyers to lead capture page
  - Put everyone that responds on Buyers List
- Day 4 Post 10 Bandit signs 1 or 2 miles around the property
  - Post near convenient stores
  - Busy streets
  - Each end of the property street (nearest busy street)
  - Post at lowes, Home depot and wal mart (if near)
  - Sign should read
    - Cheap House Must Sell
    - Handy Man Special
    - Cheap Fixer upper
    - Etc
- Day 7 Run Facebook ads for Cash the cheap property
  - Run for people between 28 and 60 in surrounding area
- You Have Buyer
  - Assign your contract or sign a new contract to double close
  - $1,000 to $2,000 earnest money NON refundable
  - No inspections for Buyers
  - Talk the Assignment contract to your title company
- Close the Deal 7 to 14 days at a local title company
- Have them wire your money or send you a check

That is the process in a nutshell.

**Lets Dive in and get down to business.**

At this point, lets pretend you have a house under contract, and not what are you going to do? You should have your contract signed a 15-day inspection period and closing in 30 days or whatever is in your contract.

Remember that you are not actually buying the property when wholesaling.  Our main strategy is going to be to assign the contract.  Sometimes you will close on a property. For example, your seller needs to close today and you know it's a great deal. So you close on the property  (using transactional Funding) and then might wholesale it to another investor in a few weeks. If you are going to wholesale a bank owned property you will have to close on it. (but you can flip in right away and still make a lot of $$$)

## Finding Wholesale Buyers to gobble up your Deals

Your Goal should be to have a HUGE buyers list. Every time you have a wholesale deal, investors should be calling you like crazy. Once you have established that you provide real estate investors with amazing deals, you will not have to work hard to find a buyer.

Once you have a large buyers list you will then overtime you will start weeding it down to a small group of elite buyers.

Building Your Buyers List can be one of the easiest things. I think it is one of the easiest parts of your real estate investing Business. I have heard lots of people saying that it's hard but believe me if you have good deals, Buyers will be tracking you down.

To run a successful wholesaling business, you will need to have cash buyers. If you have 5 good wholesale buyers who pay all cash and can close quickly, you can make tons of money wholesaling.

So who are your buyers? Other Investors, Rehabbers, Landlords, and anyone who wants to pay all cash for a house. Now that you know who you are looking for where, do you think these people would hang out?

**Your Local REIA**

The First Place to look is at your Local Real Estate Investors Association. Most cities and towns have one and they usually meet once a month. You can Google Your Area and REIA to find one. You can also go to http://www.nationalreia.com/

The REIA is a Great Place to start building your buyers list; you will have all kinds of investors at the REIA. Make Sure You Bring Your Business Cards and Hand them Out to Everyone. Get everyone's cards and tell them you are finding tons of cheap houses right now. Ask them if they would be interested in being added to your buyers list.

Become Best friends with the President of the REIA, they have the list and names of all the members. You could have the President Blast your Deals out to hundreds or thousands of investors. Think About it.

I have always asked investors what type of houses they are looking for, areas, and what the maximum price they will pay. Most of them will usually tell me anything if it's a deal. Try and get more specific with them, and say ok if I bring you anything that is a deal and will you buy it? And maybe they will then get a little more specific.

If you can really narrow down what investors are looking for, it will help you figure out what kinds of houses to put under contract.

## The Court House Steps

The next place to find Buyers is Foreclosure auctions. When buying properties at foreclosure auction, you are required to have a cashier's check or proof of funds. What that means is that anyone bidding on property at the auction has cash to buy properties.

Investors at these auctions are looking to buy cheap property and make money. After the Auction or prior to the auction, talk to these people and tell them you are a wholesaler and ask if they would be interested in Cheap Properties.

If you are doing deals in other markets you will want to either pay someone to go down to the court house and hand out flyers for you or have your wholesaler go to the court house on auction day and hand out flyers.

## Run Classified Ads

I usually post a classified ad every day or so on Craigslist.org.

The only time I post classified ads is when I have a deal under contract. I just put something like "Steal this super cheap house from me" and then a little bit about the property. In craigslist I personally do not give out the address until they email me and I don't put any pictures. This way if your seller starts browsing craiglsit they will not see their house being sold.

I seem to get a buyer or two to join every time I post an ad.

## Freedomsoft

Freedomsoft-4.com has a section where you can pull all of the cash buyers for your area. They compile data from recent houses that have sold for all cash. All you have to do is hit the search button and BOOM, you instantly have cash buyers. You can then contact these people to buy your house. Go to **http://freedomsoft-4.com** for more info and to get your free trial.

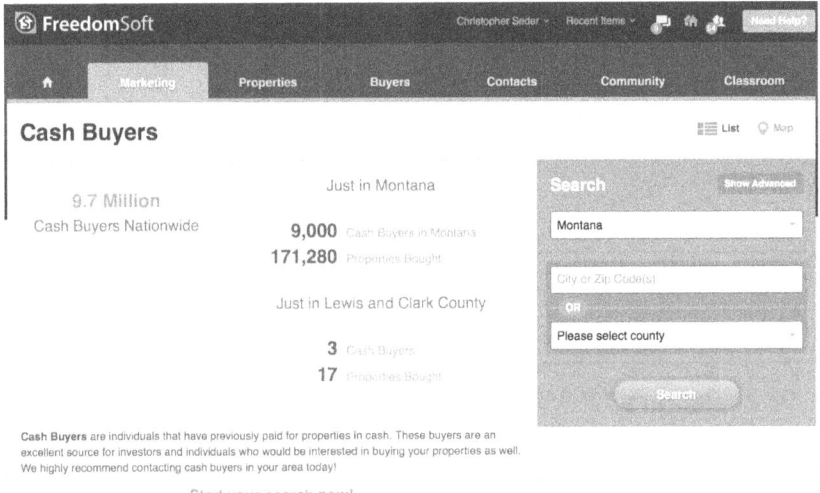

## The Realtor's MLS

Because the first step in the process is to have a realtor pull all of the cash sales for you, you already have access to all of the cash sales from the MLS. This is what I call pure gold. Now what you will have to do is look up each of the houses on the local tax assessor's office and find the owners name.

Then what you can do is either search their name in Google or use a skip tracing web site like TLO.com to find their contact info.    This will be by far one of the most effective ways for you to start finding cash buyers.

Another TIP with MLS Cash Sales.  If you have all of the cash sales pulled and you currently have all of the Selling agents info in the cash sales (phone or email), you can simply start calling all of the realtors up and tell them you have a property you are selling for 50% below market value and wondering if they have a cash buyer that might be interested?  Tell them to just add their commission to the top of your asking price (example your selling for $40,000 they add $2,000 and market to their buyer for $42,000).

Some of the best cash buyers will come from selling agents and you need to be able to work with these people.

**Find Cash Buyers NOW**

Ok so another great tool I have mentioned before is Find Cash Buyers NOW.

Go to http://virtualflips.com/cash-buyers/

This is a tool I use in my business pretty much every month.  It allows you to pull cash buyer sales and the cool thing about it is that on around 20% of them there is a phone number attached.  So all you have to do then is call them up and see if they are interested in buying more in that area.

# Wholesaling a House with no Buyers List

What if you do not have a list right now but you have a wholesale deal? Here are a few things that you can do to find wholesale buyer leads and sell your house.

**First thing to do:**

**Put out bandit signs (not in the front yard)**

Put bandit signs all over the neighborhood and at all the major stop signs near the property. Do not put the address, just put "cheap house for sale" "Fixer Upper" "Wholesale Property" or something like that and your phone number.

You will want to have your boots on the ground follow this step and paper the area with signs. I have sold a ton of houses when I first got started using simple bandit signs all over the area.

**1. Put an Ad Up on Craigslist and BackPage**

You can make simple little professional looking flyers by using sites like Postlets.com or V Flyer.

**2. Run an Ad in your local Paper**

**3.Put your Ad on Other Sites Like (Zillow.com, Truila.com, Cyberhomes.com, Homes.com)**

## 5.Put your House on Your Blog and Web Site

I use freedomsoft and wordpress to post the houses I have for sale. Get a free trial of freedomsoft-4.com if you need a nice website to post houses on.

## 6.Take your Deal to Your Local Real Estate Club President

Every city or most have a local real estate investing association and the president of that club has a buyer's list of hundreds or thousands. Find the REIA nearest you and call the president. Tell them you have a killer deal and were wondering if they knew of any members looking for what you have.

## 7. Start running facebook ads.

An amazing place to find buyers is on facebook. I have sold a ton of houses by running facebook ads. Now facebook ads can be very tricky at first and I recommend you purchase Digital Marketers $7 Facebook ads course go to DigitalMarketer.com and search for it.

If you do not advertise correctly you will just be wasting money. I could honestly go into an entire book just on facebook ads but for now I don't want to bore you.

When running an ad you will need a web page (typically a squeeze page to capture leads) and also you will need to create ads that get peoples attention. An awesome place to create graphics and ad designs is Canva.com.

## 8. Joint venture with another wholesaler

Now if worse comes to worse and you just cannot find anyone you may need to call in another local wholesaler. What I would then do is offer that wholesaler 30% of the wholesale fee. My other wholesalers cut would get cut back to 20% (if I have it under contract) and I would still get my 50% wholesale fee.

Now you will have buyers contacting you like crazy. Remember we are just putting a motivated seller together with a motivated buyer.

**You are going to get several different types of buyers calling you.**

- Some will just ask you for the address and say thanks.
- Some will ask you tons of questions.
- Some will want to see the inside of the property and want to set up a time to meet you.

Other buyers will make you an offer right there and then. One thing to remember is that if we are wholesaling the property, it's going to be hard to walk tons of buyers through the house. We should have told the seller and put in a contingency that we are able to walk inspectors and partners through the property. If you have several people that want to see the property before they make an offer, we need to pre-screen them first.

The best way to pre-screen is to tell them this is a cash sale or hard money sell only and ask if they could email or fax you their proof of funds. Some buyers will not like this. Once you have found a few cash buyers that are interested, call up your seller and set up a time to walk them through the house. Before you go to the property with your buyer, tell them that you have the property under contract right now and that they need to present themselves as either one of your partners or inspectors. If they deviate from this plan, we will not be able to do business anymore.

**We want the buyers who make offers right away**

To determine if we are talking to good Wholesale Buyers, we have to evaluate our buyer. Making sure your wholesale buyer is serious and this is why pre-screening them is very important. You will waste lots of valuable time messing around with unqualified buyers.

When you first meet or talk with a buyer, you want to gather as much information as you can. You need to make sure your buyer actually has the money to buy your wholesale property. Ask how they close on property. Do they use Cash, Hard Money, Financing, or Private Money? You also need to know how fast they can close on a property. Do not always take the buyers word that they can pay all cash. Ask if they can get you a proof of funds from their bank, I let them know that I will require one.

Another good thing to know is how experienced they are. Experienced investors can really make the process run smoothly.

Also when talking with buyers its important that if THEY do not want your deal that you ask them questions WHY? Ask them at what price they would buy it? What their thoughts where? And try to gather everything you can from your buyers in regards to their buying criteria. Some buyers are just time wasters and will never buy a property from you. They are waiting for that perfect deal which does not exist.

## How to Choose Between Multiple Offers

Cash is the business we want to be in because it makes deals easier to close and go faster. If I am choosing between different offers on a property, I will always look for offers that are all cash terms first.

If you go with someone looking to finance the property, you will spend countless of weeks with the seller calling you asking when you are going to close and you having to chase the buyer around asking him or her. It will become a mess. If you can avoid it, only deal with cash buyers.

Just use your judgment to determine which offer you want to accept. Look for closing date (how fast they can close), terms, and pick one you like best.

## Assign the Contract

After you choose your offer, simply fill out an assignment contract with your buyer. Take the contract and assignment to the title company or your closing attorney and your job is done. Just tell the title company to start the title process.

When assigning a contract we always get a $1,000 to $2,000 NON refundable earnest money deposit from the buyer. This earnest money either goes directly to our company or goes to the title company. Never assign one of your deals without an earnest money deposit.

### Sometimes you will have to Double Close

Every once in a while you will want to do what is called a double close. This is where you close on the property (using transactional funding) and you turn around and sell it to your buyer the same day.

If your buying from a bank you will want to do a double close or sometimes if your going to be making over $10,000 it's a good idea to do a double close. If a buyer knows your making a lot on the deal they will sometimes try and strong-arm you into taking less. But if you have built a relationship with them and sold them lots of deals then I would not worry about double closing.

**The Typical Closing Process**

I want to add this little section on the closing process just to make you understand everything with closing a real estate deal.

When closing a real estate deal we close the deal at a local title company or closing attorney. Typically the first step happens once you put the property under contract with the seller. You will then bring the purchase and sale agreement along with an earnest money deposit to the title company and tell them to start the title work. Also tell them you may be assigning your contract and ask if there is any documentation you will need from them in order to do that.

Some title companies will require you do have the sellers sign an agreement before or at closing just stating the fact that you assigned the contract. The title company will also need all of your business info you have like your articles of organization, EIN number or your Social Security Number.

Once you have the contract at the title company lets jump to the part where NOW you have a buyer lined up and you have signed an assignment agreement with them. You will want to provide your buyer with a copy of the Original Purchase and sale agreement you signed with the seller and a copy of the assignment.    Then take the original assignment over to the title company (or email) and tell them you have assigned the contract.

A good title company will know what to do and process all of the title work now with the new buyers info.

From this point on you will just wait to make sure the title is clear of leans and then wait for the title company to schedule a closing data with the buyer and seller.   Make sure you are checking in with the title company a couple times a week to see if there is anything else you need to be doing or anything they need from you.   From this point your job is pretty much done and all you have to do is sit back and make sure the deal closes and make sure your buyer and seller are happy.

**Note:** I wont get into this too much but sometimes you are going to run across problems where there is a Lien on the property, which could cause some problems.   We come across Tax liens, IRS liens, child support liens and so on.   You will want to work with the Title Company and seller to figure out what the best solution is to solve the problem.   Sometimes this may mean cutting your wholesale fee down a bit to make everything work or sometimes it will kill the deal.  Just remember there is always a solution to every problem and its your job to figure it out.

**Keys To Remember….**

Buyers are everywhere and every buyer is not created equally.   I like to work with buyers that make my life easier by closing quickly; paying all cash and NOT negotiating down my price.  These are the best and will make your life easier.   I also have built up a good solid friendship with a lot of my buyers who trust my judgment and who I like to do business with.

Also remember that when doing deals virtually you want to work with an experienced wholesaler who already have cash buyers waiting for cheap houses.  This one step right there will make your life a whole lot easier and you will never have to worry about even building a buyers list in another market.

Now get out and Flip a House or continue reading this book, either choice is going to make you some money.

# Notes:

# Chapter 8: Creating a Kick Ass Virtual Flips Business

"I value self-discipline, but creating systems that make it next to impossible to misbehave is more reliable than self-control"
-Tim Ferriss

"I would rather earn 1% off a 100 people's efforts than 100% of my own efforts"
-John D. Rockefeller

The goal with Virtual flips is to after a few months of hard work, creating relationships, setting up new real estate markets is to have a virtual flips business that runs on almost autopilot.   With my virtual flips business we are in several different real estate markets and flip several houses each month.  The good thing about my business is that I DO not needs to really do much to run it.  If I want go on vacation I can hand over the reigns to my acquisitions manager and he can handle all of our wholesale deals and we would still have money coming in each month.

The great thing about real estate wholesaling is that you can automate just about every aspect of the business. From Market research, finding deals, and even closing deals. Its not rocket science it just takes a little bit of work to get all of the pieces put in place.

## Outsourcing Your Business

In order to run your business and not work in your business you need to start outsourcing everything you possibly can.

**The first thing** that I recommend you outsource is your marketing and what I mean by that is that you use sites like click2mail.com to send out your post cards instead of doing them your self.

I do not recommend you outsource the pulling of mailing lists and creating your marketing campaign until you have done a lot of deals and have it down. This is HUGE because just the simplest error in uploading your mailing lists, sorting them and picking the correct mailing list can cost you thousands.

But once you do have it down, document everything you do and create a screen shot video of exactly how you pull your mailing lists, sort them and upload them.   Once that is all created you can simply have your acquisitions manager do all of this for you.

**The Second thing** I recommend you outsource is your in bound calls.   By having a site like patlive.com takes all of your incoming phone calls and pre-screening them you can save a lot of time.   I will never go back to answering my own phone calls again.   When setting up pat live use "Ron Legrand" as a promo code to receive a nice discount.

**The third thing** you will want to outsource is evaluating deals and making offers.  This step comes once you have done several deals and pretty much have the wholesaling process down.  What you will want to do is create an easy to follow screen shot video of your process for evaluating deals.

Something a lazy high school kid could easily follow and put the houses through a formula to come up with your Max offer price.

Once you get to this point I recommend you hire an Acquisitions Manager who can do this for you. Their job will be to call back all of the sellers, and make them offers.

Your acquisitions manager's job will be to do all of the leg work necessary to get a property under contract, this includes looking at houses, taking pictures, meeting and negotiating with sellers and signing contracts.

**The forth thing** you need to be outsourcing is your entire buyer marketing. Again like any step in the process you will want to do everything you can to build up a buyers list of ACTUAL cash buyers and putting in the legwork to find them. Once you have the process down and have compiled an email list of a lot of them, wholesaled several houses you can easily automate this process.

If I am wholesaling houses in my own town I can simply make 5 phone calls and the house is SOLD. If your doing it virtually your wholesaler you are working with combined with your acquisitions manager will handle everything when it comes to finding buyers.

**The Firth thing** you need to start outsourcing is your NEW city market research. Once you have proven that your process works and you have done market research in several new markets its not time to have someone like your acquisitions manager do more leg work and start finding new markets to go into.

Market research is pretty easy to do and even easier to outsource but I think its one of the pieces that as a business owner you should always be somewhat involved in. Picking the wrong real estate market and wrong area can be a terrible business decision.

| City Name | State Name | City Population | MSA Population | Low Price | 50th Price | Low Rent | 50th Rent | Eqivalent Supply | Eqivalent Demand | P-Ratio | Add To MyCities |
|---|---|---|---|---|---|---|---|---|---|---|---|
| Philadelphia | PA | 1,547,607 | 6,018,800 | $1,250 | $16,000 | $0 | $0 | 51,507 | 1,045 | 8.41 | Add |
| Phoenix | AZ | 1,468,750 | 4,329,534 | $29,000 | $40,000 | $0 | $0 | 10,749 | 2,145 | 6.04 | Add |
| Pittsburgh | PA | 306,211 | 2,359,733 | $1,500 | $11,000 | $0 | $0 | 12,004 | 208 | 45.21 | Add |
| Portland | OR | 603,106 | 2,289,600 | $29,000 | $114,950 | $0 | $0 | 10,943 | 4,974 | 2.21 | Add |
| San Antonio | TX | 1,352,951 | 2,234,000 | $14,000 | $93,000 | $0 | $0 | 8,315 | 1,176 | 7.25 | Add |
| San Diego | CA | 1,338,348 | 3,177,063 | $7,000 | $230,000 | $0 | $0 | 3,735 | 762 | 4.91 | Add |
| Seattle | WA | 634,535 | 3,562,137 | $67,000 | $107,000 | $0 | $0 | 7,879 | 3,057 | 2.58 | Add |
| St. Louis | MO | 318,172 | 2,795,794 | $1,000 | $3,900 | $0 | $0 | 32,749 | 4,314 | 6.95 | Add |
| Tampa | FL | 549,543 | 2,842,478 | $7,000 | $78,000 | $0 | $0 | 51,726 | 7,478 | 6.93 | Add |
| Washington | DC | 633,323 | 5,840,342 | $30,000 | $385,000 | $0 | $0 | 16,289 | 2,609 | 6.25 | Add |

Now there will be other small things that you will want to out source but for now that is all you really need to do. As you can see outsourcing does not mean passing off everything to a Virtual Assistant or someone who does not have a vested interest in your business. It means outsourcing to your KICK ass team you have put together and empowering them with more and more responsibility as you grow.

## Virtual Flips Business Structure

In every good business you want grow it to the point where you are on top as CEO, the owner, President or what ever it might be.

When starting out your job is going to be CEO, Marketing manager and your own acquisitions manager. Once you have all of the systems in place and are making money then you can expand to filling other positions. Also you do not need salary employees unless you are making upwards of $500,000 per year. I personally do not have anyone on salary and pretty much just pay everyone a % of deals that come in. But it's your world when creating a business and you can structure it however you like.

Below is a Map Graphic of several of the positions I have. They may be a little fuzzy but it should give you a good idea or what each person should be doing.

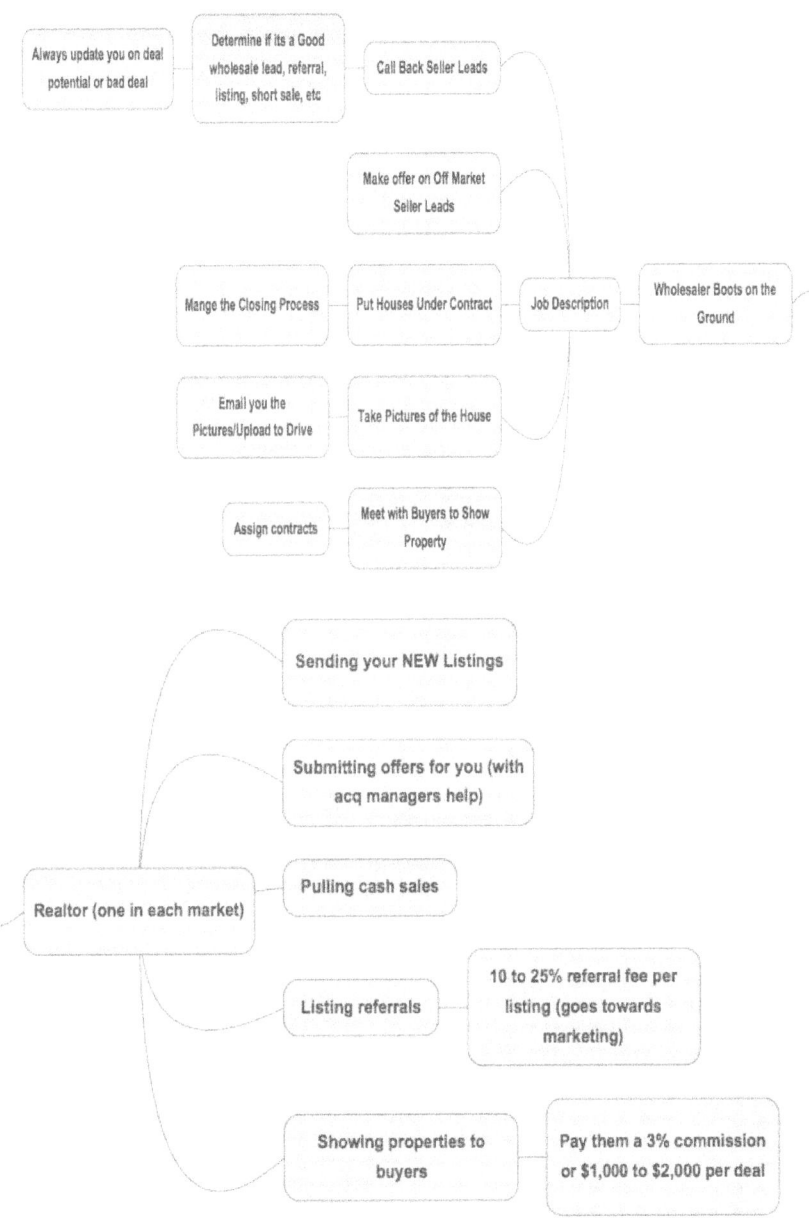

Always update you on deal potential or bad deal

Determine if its a Good wholesale lead, referral, listing, short sale, etc

Call Back Seller Leads

Make offer on Off Market Seller Leads

Mange the Closing Process

Put Houses Under Contract

Job Description

Wholesaler Boots on the Ground

Email you the Pictures/Upload to Drive

Take Pictures of the House

Assign contracts

Meet with Buyers to Show Property

Sending your NEW Listings

Submitting offers for you (with acq managers help)

Pulling cash sales

Realtor (one in each market)

Listing referrals

10 to 25% referral fee per listing (goes towards marketing)

Showing properties to buyers

Pay them a 3% commission or $1,000 to $2,000 per deal

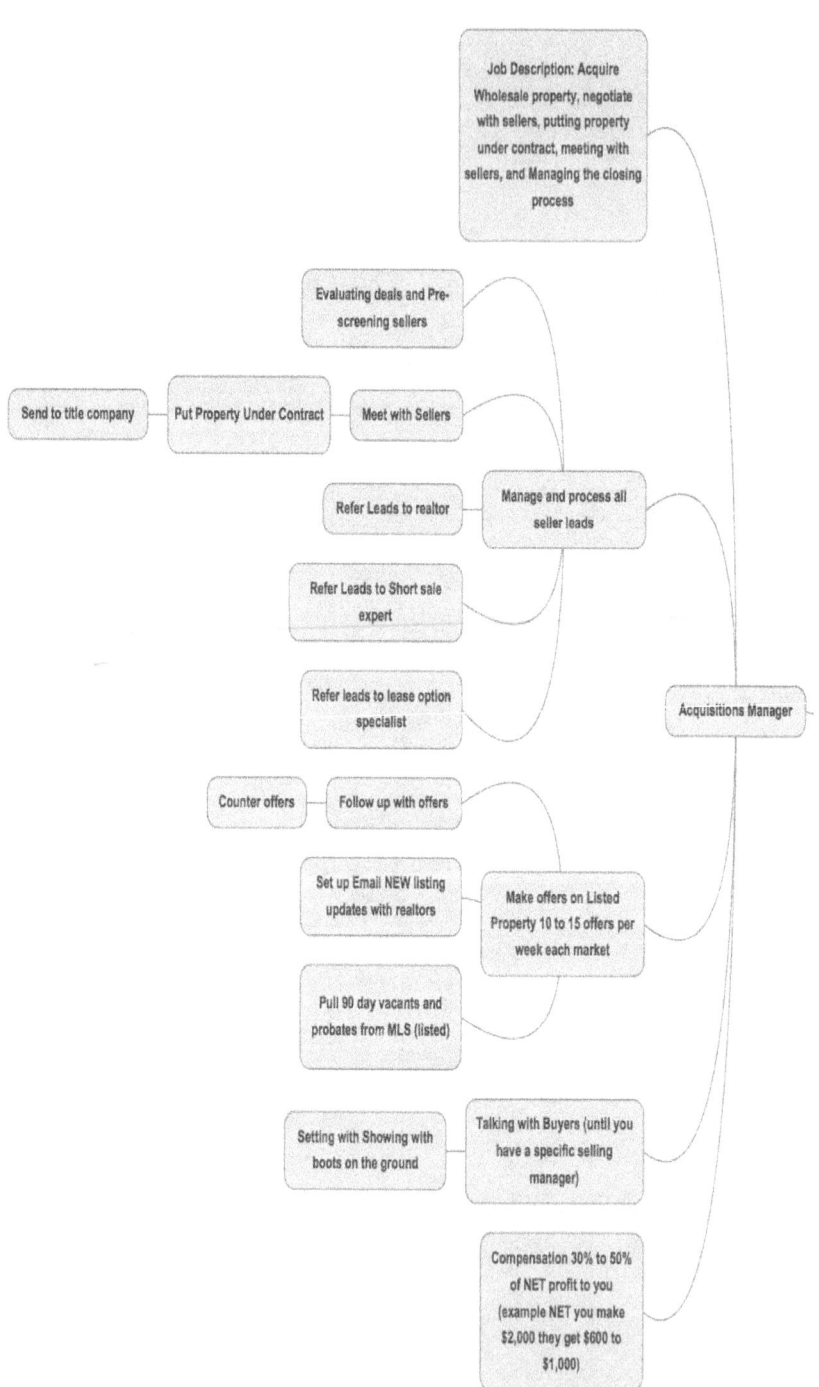

Job Description: Acquire Wholesale property, negotiate with sellers, putting property under contract, meeting with sellers, and Managing the closing process

Evaluating deals and Pre-screening sellers

Send to title company — Put Property Under Contract — Meet with Sellers

Refer Leads to realtor — Manage and process all seller leads

Refer Leads to Short sale expert

Refer leads to lease option specialist

Acquisitions Manager

Counter offers — Follow up with offers

Set up Email NEW listing updates with realtors — Make offers on Listed Property 10 to 15 offers per week each market

Pull 90 day vacants and probates from MLS (listed)

Setting with Showing with boots on the ground — Talking with Buyers (until you have a specific selling manager)

Compensation 30% to 50% of NET profit to you (example NET you make $2,000 they get $600 to $1,000)

Remember when hiring anyone to be on your team you want to hire slow and fire quickly. I have a no dip shits policy in my business. If you are not an A player, go getter, hustler and all around cool person then you will not be working with me. I only wan to work with the best.

## Virtual Flips Revenue Goals

If you want to actually run a business and NOT a hobby you need to know what its actually going to take in order to achieve your business goals. Below I have included a Wholesaling revenue goals spread sheet picture.

You can download the actual spreadsheet inside the full virtual flips online course.

What this spread sheet does is allow you to put in HOW much you want to make wholesaling this year and it will show you what kind of volume you need to be doing. Its pretty cool and really lays out ACTUAL numbers and not some fairy tail.

# 2015 Wholesaling Revenue Goals

| | | |
|---|---|---|
| Annual Revenue | $ | 500,000 |
| Weekly Revenue | $ | 9,615 |
| Monthly Revenue | $ | 41,667 |

| | |
|---|---|
| Average Profit Per deal | $7,000 |
| Average JV Profit 50% | $3,500.0 |
| Virtual Flips JV Profit | |

| | |
|---|---|
| Annual Deals needed (Self) | 71 |
| JV Deals Needed | 143 |

| | |
|---|---|
| Leads to produce 1 deal | 30 |
| Mailers to Get 30 leads 3% | 1,000 |

| | |
|---|---|
| Annual Leads Needed DM | 2,143 |
| Monthly marketing Sent | 5,952 |
| Annual Marketing Sent | 71,429 |

| | | |
|---|---|---|
| Annual Marketing Budget | $ | 35,714.29 |
| Cost Per lead | $ | 16.67 |

| | |
|---|---|
| JV Leads Needed | 4,286 |
| (note work half the time) | |
| Monthly marketing Sent | 11,905 |
| Annul Marketing Sent | 142,857 |

| | | |
|---|---|---|
| Cost of Marketing | $ | 71,428.57 |
| Cost Per lead | $ | 16.67 |

| | |
|---|---|
| Hours work per deal(self) | 20 |
| Total Hours Worked | 1428.57 |
| Hours per week | 27.47 |

| | |
|---|---|
| JV Hours Work per deal | 2 |
| JV Hours Work Total | 285.71 |
| Hour Per week | 5.49 |

| | | | |
|---|---|---|---:|
| | **Expenses (self)** | | |
| | Acquisitions Manager (25%) | $ | 125,000.00 |
| | Office Expense | | |
| | Freedomsoft | $ | 1,164.00 |
| | Voice Mail | $ | 600.00 |
| | Office Supplies | $ | 2,000.00 |
| | Cost of Marketing | $ | 35,714.29 |
| | **Net Revenue (self)** | $ | **335,521.71** |
| | | | |
| | **Expenses Virtual JV Deals** | | |
| | Acquisition Manager | $ | 125,000.00 |
| | Office Expenses | $ | 3,764.00 |
| | Marketing Expense | $ | 71,428.57 |
| | **Net RevenueVirtual JV** | $ | **299,807.43** |
| | | | |
| Extra Expense | **Pat Live** | | |
| Optional | Free Minutes | | 3,000 |
| | Phone Calls 4 min each | | 8571.43 |
| | Total Paid Mins | | 5,571 |
| | Cost of Pat Live Per year | $ | 1,800.00 |
| | Plus Overage Mins | $ | 5,571.43 |
| | **Total Cost** | $ | **7,371.43** |
| | (saves Ac Manager Time) | | |
| | | | |
| Comparing | | | |
| | Net Income Self Deals | $ | 335,521.71 |
| | Net weekly Income | $ | 6,452.34 |
| | Monthly Income | $ | 27,960.14 |
| | Hours Per week Worked | | 27.47 |
| | **Revenue Per hour** | $ | **234.87** |
| | | | |
| | Net Income JV Deals | $ | 299,807.43 |
| | Net Weekly Income | $ | 5,765.53 |
| | Net Monthly Income | $ | 24,983.95 |
| | Hours per week worked | | 5.49 |
| | **Revenue Per hour** | $ | **1,049.33** |

From the spread sheet you can see that if you want to generate $500,000 in revenue this year doing ONLY virtual flips you are going to need to do around 143 deals. I know what your thinking that is a lot of deals but as you can also see that if you set up your virtual flips business correctly you will only need to be working around 5 ½ hours per week. They key in this is setting up your team and having a good acquisitions manager in place that can handle all of th work load for you.

With this spread sheet I didn't want to sugar coat anything and tell you that you can do this with NO money, or anything. As you can see its going to take marketing DOLLARS and to get it to the 143 deal per year point you are going to need to put in some HARD work. But once you put all of the pieces in place your life is going to change forever.

**Final Thoughts on automating your business**

When automating and growing your business you MUST write down everything you do in your business to create systems that you can easily hand to an acquisitions manager and he can follow the steps, implement them and have success.

In order to create systems in your business you must first DO everything yourself.  Even if its just doing everything a couple times to get a feel for it that's ok.  And this is exactly WHY I created the Virtual Flips course so that I have step-by-step videos my team can easily follow and have success.   Heck if you do not want to screen record all of the steps you can simply give your acquisitions manager the Virtual flips course and have them watch all of the videos and implement them.

You also want to create your own goals in your business.  Remember if you want to make lets say $100,000 this year wholesaling in other markets you need to know exactly HOW many deals you need to do and exactly how many marketing pieces you need to send out.  If you do not know this you will most likely fail.

# Notes:

# Chapter 9: Your Master Plan

"Make a lot of fast, recoverable mistakes and you'll prevent most of the fatal ones."
**-Tim Ferris -4 Hour Work Week**

In this last official chapter of Virtual Flips I want to make sure you have everything you need in order to go out and conquer the real estate wholesaling world.

As you can see from the overall virtual flips process you can easily flip houses virtually from the comfort of your own home and once you have a system in place there is no easier strategy to make an extra $7,000 this month or create that 4 hour work week life style you want.

Wither you are going to be wholesaling houses virtually or wholesaling in your own back yard you can create a well oiled machine that brings in deals each and every week.

So what are some key take always from this book?

**Market Research Rules**.  No matter what kind of real estate investing you are doing you must know the real estate market you will be doing business in.   If you do not know the very best areas to wholesale houses in, rehab houses, etc then you are going to make your life more difficult.

**A Trustworthy Team is Key**.   In order to run your business successful you must have others you can trust in key positions to help you grow and take the work load off of you.   Remember to always be skeptical when looking to partner with someone.  Be slow to hire and quick to fire.

**Market or Die**.  No matter what kind of business you are in if you are not generating leads and turning them into sales then your business is dying.   Make sure you are consistently sending out direct mail each and every month.

**Use Technology and Expertise**.  When pre-screening leads us all of the technology you can in order to make your life easier.   Remember to use the experience of other wholesalers in the market you are wholesaling in to help determine if it's a deal or no deal.

**Buyers are the Easy Part.**  If you have a deal (an actual deal not some over priced piece of crap) buyers will flood to you.   No matter what real estate market you are in if you have a good enough deal you will have buyers flooding to do business with you and by following a few easy steps you can find a flood of them waiting to give you cash.

**5 Offers a Day Keeps the Bill Collector Away**.  The only way you are going to have success is by actively making a crap ton of offers.   Do not half ass this step. The amount of offers you make will be directly correlated to the amount of money you make.

If your have been trying to get started for months or years I challenge you to be honest with yourself and look at HOW many offers you have made over the past 2 or 3 months?  Don't make up some bull crap excuse either be honest, HOW many written offers? If its less than 20 offers then you have your answer to why you are not successful.

**Build a Business that runs itself.**  The end goal of any business you build is to create something that will one day run itself.  Your job needs to be to master every aspect of your business so that down the road you can outsource everything and just manage your team.  Total 4 hour work week lifestyle. Its not going to happen over night and it actually took me years to put all of the pieces together but just keep at it and your time will come.

The Virtual Flips process is not complicated and DO not make it overly complicated. If your scared to do it virtually start in your own local market, get some experience and then branch out. You can apply all of the principals learned in the book to your own local market or any market across the country.

**Before I finish this chapter lets get real..**
In this book I have not really touched on one of the most important aspects of your success. This aspect is going to single handedly determine if you are going to make it with real estate investing. It's more important than any real estate investing strategy on the planet. Now I know you have probably already guessed what it is. It's your mindset.

No matter what sort of business you are in if you truly want to be successful you need to first cultivate the mindset of success. You need to not only have a good positive attitude but you need to develop the mindset that nothing is going to stop you, nothing is going to get you down, and every obstacle put in your bath is there to make you stronger.

Now I could probably write an entire chapter on mindset and how to become super human but I am not going to do that. I just want to get you thinking about it and refer you to some of the people and books that have changed my life and continue to help me grow stronger every day.

So to start off if you do not already know of Preston Ely you need to get to know him. He is the guy who set my mind on fire back in 2009 when I was first getting started. I read everything he was posting, read all of his recommended books and it helped me develop what I consider a millionaire real estate investor mindset. You can check out a bunch of his free blog postings on WakeWealthy.com

The next person you need to start reading about and all about his books is of course Napoleon Hill and his Think and Grow Rich book. This is by far the best book out there on how to start accumulating a better mindset and becoming wealthier. Get that book and read it.

Another great book is T Harv Ekers The millionaire mind. It's a very easy ready and will change your thoughts and beliefs on how millionaires think. Get that book and read it.

And of course if you have not read the 4-Hour Workweek by Tim Ferris go out and get that book right away. It may just change your life.

Ok so those are three people who I think can inspire you to start becoming a better you. There are hundreds of other books out there but just learn to develop a habit of reading at least on book on mindset and positive thinking at least once a month if not more.

That is all she wrote for this chapter, I will see you in the Bonus chapter.

Remember to get out and Implement all of the steps we discussed. You are NOW on your journey to becoming a **Virtual House Flipping Machine.**

# Bonus Chapter: Virtual Flips

## Virtual Flips Proudly Presents

The Smartest, Fastest, and Absolute Best way to get started Virtual Wholesaling. Period.

**Disclaimer:** If you are looking for a magic pill that will make you a sexy virtual flipping machine then you are in the wrong place. If you are looking to work your butt off, and follow a step-by-step proven process then you are in the right place.

Perhaps you have asked yourself this question before, "Self, why do I work 40, 50, 80 hours per week building a big pile of cash for someone else?" No doubt yourself answered back saying "because you're just scared to break away from the man and go out on your own" or "because real estate you're just not good enough" or "Real Estate investing is too hard"

I know this because I have been there before. I told myself every excuse in the book as to why I was not making the kind of money I wanted to be with real estate.

But I am here to tell you, if I can do it. You can too break free and start living the life of your dreams with wholesaling and Virtual Wholesaling.

If you want to become a rock start virtual flipper you need to cultivate the attitude that you are a champion and nothing is going to stop you from success. Stop believing the negative thoughts you are having and start correcting those thoughts.

One of the biggest hurdles for most people is fear of getting started before they have all the answers. Let me tell you that you do not have to know everything to get going and sometimes its best to just dive in headfirst. But if you do have some reservations about diving in without knowing how to swim I don't blame you and that is one reason why I wrote this book just for you and why I created the VirtualFlips.com digital course.

I have taken my exact virtual flips process and laid it out in video form that is easy for anyone to follow. Every question that you could possibly ask is all covered in a simple how to video.

I had to struggle to learn the virtual flips business and it took me a while to develop a system that works but I have done that. If you want to learn how to start living the life of your dreams and learn how to have piles of cold hard cash flowing into your life each and every month then you should check out the course.

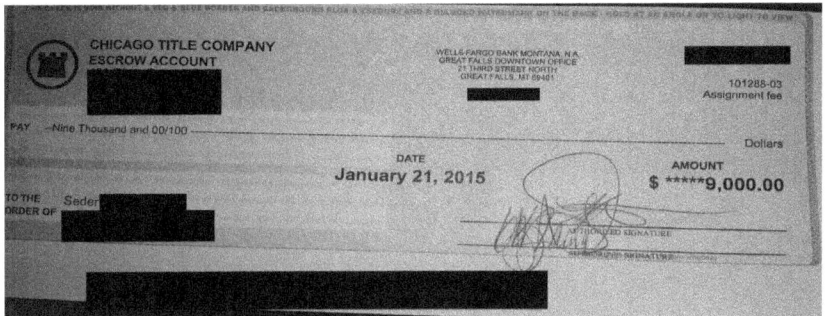

(Actual $9,000 check from a virtual Flip, my work on this deal was around 45 mins, cha ching)

Listen, I'm not bragging here. People may accuse me of flaunting deals we are closing but I don't care. My goal is to inspire you to see what is truly possible because once you believe it that is when you will start to realize you can do it.


## Virtual Flips Success Key

*You will seldom improve your situation if you do not have a simple process to copy. Why? Because you are lazy and the copy paste button is just easier.*

**The 3 things YOU NEED in order to succeed…**
I attribute to most of my success to a combination of having a good solid mentor, developing a proven system and having a winning mindset. With these three things you can accomplish anything you set your mind to.

I personally do the exact same process I have taught you in this book and teach in the Virtual Flips full online course. It has proven to create a consistent income for myself each and every month.

If you want to Be Successful with real estate wholesaling, start learning and hanging out with Successful wholesaler's and real estate investors. All of my friends I associate with are young successful people. .

They are on their way to the top. Most of us live all across the country but the one thing we have in common is a passion for learning and growing.

**Virtual Flips Success Key**
*"If you want to get out of your current situation you need to take MASSIVE action and do what is necessary but not always what is easiest"*

Bottom line- hand around losers who talk about how much they hate their boss, how much their life sucks, and how sorry their life is and soon you will start talking the same way. You will find your self not only broke but a miserable person. But if you start hanging around me and my friends you will soon realize that anything is possible when it comes to life and business.

**Want to take your Virtual Wholesaling business to the next level?**

Remember virtual wholesaling is not complicated you have seen the entire process laid out in this book. But there still are a lot of working pieces and questions most people have.

If you're like me you're a visual learner, and the best way I learn is by seeing. This is why I have put all of my systems and processes into easy to follow videos. Not only do you see everything laid out but you also hear it.

So pay close attention, because this is NOT like most regular house flipping programs.

# The Virtual Flips Course

**What it is NOT**: A starting point to get you to move into a higher level course and give you just enough to get you motivated.

**What it is:** It's a step-by-step, all-inclusive course designed to take you from zero to hero in no time. Think you have learned a lot just from this book? Think about HOW much more you will learn in the full virtual flips course.

**What you get?**

**6 Core modules** that goes through our entire virtual wholesaling process step by step in easy to follow videos.
These core modules will take you from Market Research, Building your team, marketing, evaluating, and finding buyers and getting paid.

# We will also show you how you can start developing your virtual flips business so you can enjoy the 4 hour workweek life style.

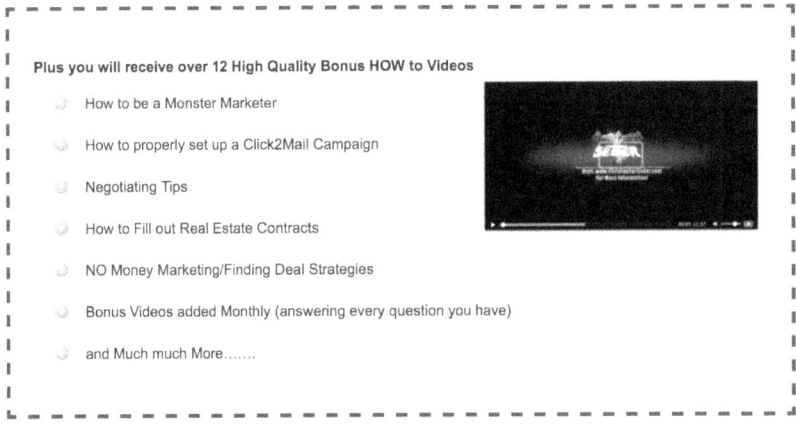

Plus you will receive over 12 High Quality Bonus HOW to Videos

- How to be a Monster Marketer
- How to properly set up a Click2Mail Campaign
- Negotiating Tips
- How to Fill out Real Estate Contracts
- NO Money Marketing/Finding Deal Strategies
- Bonus Videos added Monthly (answering every question you have)
- and Much much More.......

Plus you are getting all of the <u>forms</u>, <u>documents</u> and <u>marketing material</u> you need to become a fully-functional Virtual Wholesaler:

- ✅ Real Estate Contracts (purchase and sale, assignment, etc)
- ✅ Repair Estimate Form
- ✅ Wholesaling Joint Venture Form (make sure you get paid)
- ✅ My High Converting Seller Post Card
- ✅ NEW marketing material (new tests)
- ✅ PLUS HOW to Videos on how to fill everything out and do everything
- ✅ and Much Much More....

## Plus Receive my HIGH converting Post card…

This post card recently brought in over a **12% response rate** on 1 mailing campaign.    It works amazing.  (note: its a yellow post card with Amazing copy writing aka words that make people want to call you)  Typically pulls in around a 5% response rate which is better than industry average.

If you want to make a change in your life today I encourage you to implement what you have learned in this book and go out and make it happen. Right now is the very best time in history to get started Wholesaling houses in your own market or across the country.

If you need help the Virtual Flips course is full of amazing info that is going to Jump-start your success and give you the extra boost of confidence you need in order to get out and make it happen with real estate investing.

## 100 Mailers Sent (tax lien)

- Purchased for $24,000
- Sold to another investor for $35,000
- Total Profit after closing expenses $10,000

**THE VIRTUAL FLIPS course is designed to take you step by step through our entire process.**

There has never been a better time than today to get started wholesaling houses all across the country. All you need is a little hard work, knowledge and the right system.

**If you're Ready to Get Started with the FULL virtual flips program to:**

# http://VirtualFlips.com/VF-Order

• • • • • • • • • • • • • • • • • • • • • •

# Enter Promo Code:

**AMAZON**
**AND TO RECEIVE $50 OFF YOUR PURCHASE**

• • • • • • • • • • • • • • • • • • • • • •

Click the add to cart button on the page and you will be directed to a payment page where you can use the promo code.

Your life is about to change forever and your family is going to thank you for taking action and improving the quality of life of everyone around you.

www.ingramcontent.com/pod-product-compliance
Lightning Source LLC
Chambersburg PA
CBHW051904170526
45168CB00001B/241